D0699293

ANCIENT CITIES AND TEMPLES

MAYA CITIES

PLATE I—BONAMPAK. ROOM 1. Frescoes from the eastern wall and from the lower part of the northern wall, representing, below, a string of musicians, above, important personages richly clad; there are hieroglyphics between the two scenes. Above and to the left, the entrance door with its upper decoration, and, in the background, the border decorating the skirting board of the room. (Carnegie Institution of Washington, Department of Archaeology. Photo Giles G. Healey, after reproductions by Antonio Tejeda.)

MAYA CITIES

PAUL RIVET

founder of the *Musée de l'Homme*

Translated from the French by

MIRIAM and LIONEL KOCHAN

PAUL ELEK LONDON

This translation © Elek Books Limited 1960

2nd Impression 1973

Published in Great Britain by
ELEK BOOKS LIMITED
54–58 Caledonian Road, London. N1 9RN

First published in 1954 as
'Cites Maya'
Copyrights by 'Editions Albert Guillot', 1954

Printed in Great Britain
by Unwin Brothers Limited
The Gresham Press, Old Woking, Surrey, England

A member of the Staples Printing Group

CONTENTS

To my great Mexican friends

ALFONSO CASO
and
ALBERTO RUZ LHUILLIER

whose names will forever
remain linked with those of
Monte Albán and Palenque

Foreword

THIS study is not an original work. Although I have been fortunate enough to visit certain Mayan ruins: Chichén Itzá, Uxmal, Palenque, Quiriguá, I have not been able to contribute personally to the rich studies which a number of investigators have pursued with rare good fortune during the past century and increasingly so over the last fifty years. In the works of these scholars I have found the material indispensable to the writing of the pages which follow; all credit must therefore go to them. My role has only been to try to summarize their thought without deforming it, to resist the temptation to give too much detail, to retain only the essential facts and to sacrifice secondary matters, however attractive these sometimes were. I should like to be certain that I have succeeded and that my readers will feel with me all the beauty, nobility and human character of one of the greatest civilizations of the world.

A world buried beneath ruins, under the shroud of the tropical forest, has been awakened and brought back to life, thanks to such scholars as Brasseur de Bourbourg, John Lloyd Stephens, Teobert Maler, A. P. Maudslay, Désiré Charnay, Herbert J. Spinden, Thomas Athol Joyce, Thomas Gann, J. Eric Thompson, J. T. Goodman, Éduard Seler, Sylvanus G. Morley, Alberto Ruz Lhuillier, Ignacio Marquina, to mention only the most important.

The work of many of them is free from the arrogant aridity which often characterizes the writings of specialists. It throbs with deep affection for the unknown artists who, over the centuries, built pyramids and palaces, sculptured enormous blocks of stone and manifold steles, painted wonderful frescoes, inscribed the dates of their history on paper, stucco or stone, and whose immense efforts had no tomorrow. This sympathy appeared in a very particular way in Morley's work. The greatest modern specialist in Mayan civilization, he was, in a way, naturalized as a native of Yucatán by settling in the country itself, where he died on his Chenkú hacienda amidst his chosen friends. On the subject of the beautiful Tepeu ceramics Morley writes: 'Fully aware of my great prejudice in favour of the Maya and their cultural discoveries, I firmly believe that the development of the ceramic art in question is entirely local and has had its centre in the region of Tikal-Uaxactún.'

7

The chapter, full of humour, where he puts forward a list of fifty Mayan masterpieces, not only demonstrates the knowledge and taste of the author but also his exquisite sensibility and the affection he does not attempt to conceal.

I found the same emotion in Alberto Ruz Lhuillier's account of the discovery of the crypt of the Temple of the Inscriptions at Palenque: 'On June 15, 1952 we moved the great triangular slab which sealed the entrance just sufficient to allow one person to pass. Once across the threshold, the reason for the interior staircase we had cleared and explored appeared before our wonder-struck eyes: an immense secret room closed by the occupants of Palenque a thousand years ago. Apart from the calcareous formations produced by infiltration along the walls and the arch, we might have said that our first sight of the crypt was the same as that of the last Mayan priests when they left this sacred spot for the last time. But these formations made the sight even more fantastic: walls, pillars and arches seemed cut in ice, the ground shone like snow, slim stalactites hung from the roof like fragile tapestries and the heavy stalagmites were like extinguished candles in a dark chapel.'

I can but hope that this book with its enforced conciseness will retain some small part of the sensibility which impregnates the writings and accounts of the great scholars.

We must also make grateful mention of those terrible iconoclasts of Mayan evangelization who have nevertheless passed on observations without which the efforts of modern scholars would have been unsuccessful. The Bishop of Mérida, the Franciscan father Diego de Landa, was not insensible to the civilization although he hounded its religious manifestations—its very soul—with fanaticism. There is not only hatred and sectarianism in the very precise descriptions he put together. He too was entranced by the grandeur and nobility of the heretics he persecuted.

The principal modern sources on Mayan civilization are as follows:

Spinden (Herbert J.), *A Study of Maya Art*, Memoirs of the Peabody Museum of American Archaeology and Ethnology, Harvard University, Cambridge, Vol. VI, 1913.

Gann (Thomas) and Thompson (J. Eric), *The History of the Maya*, New York, 1937.

The Maya and Their Neighbours, New York and London, 1940.

Morley (Sylvanus Griswold), *The Ancient Maya*, Stanford University, California, 1947.

I

THE MAYAN PEOPLES

GEOGRAPHY

THE territory occupied by the Maya in the pre-Columbian epoch (p. 10) corresponds to the present states of Yucatán, Campeche, Tabasco, the eastern half of the state of Chiapas, the territory of Quintana Roo in the Republic of Mexico, the territory of the Republic of Guatemala except the Pacific coast, of British Honduras, and finally the western part of the Republic of Honduras. It represents about 130,000 square miles, that is to say, nearly three-fifths of the area of France.

This vast territory is enclosed on the south-west, south and south-east by a mountain chain shaped like the arc of a circle. The hollow side faces north, overlooked by volcanic peaks of heights varying from 13,600 feet (Tajumulco) to 8,400 feet (Pacaya). Four of these are still active. This vast relief frames deep valleys. One of these is traversed by the Rio Motagua running from west to east to flow into the Atlantic in the middle of the Gulf of Honduras; the other, the Rio Usumacinta, has a generally south-northerly direction and reaches the ocean in the middle of the Gulf of Mexico.

This mountainous part of the Mayan domain has an average altitude of 3,250 feet above sea level. Winters there are dry and even cold. The rainy season lasts from May to November. The forest is broken by large grasslands which predominate above the 10,000 feet level.

Partly encircled and enclosed by this mountain chain lies the plain, which covers the central part of the Department of Petén (Guatemala) and the southern half of Yucatán. Its average height is 500 feet. It is 63 miles long by 19 wide at the maximum, and bounded to the north by hills, at the foot of which runs a chain of lakes. The most important, the Lake of Peten-Itzá, is no less than 19 miles in length by 3 in width.

This plain and the hills which bound it in the north are covered by dense tropical forest. The temperature there is very high, the

9

Map of the principal centres of the Old and New Mayan Empires.

(By courtesy of the Drawing Office, *Musée de l'Homme*)

rainy season lasts from May to January, with a dry season corresponding to the months of February, March, April and May. These last months are the hottest.

The northern half of Yucatán, which constitutes the third natural region of the Mayan domain, is characterized by considerably less vigorous and less dense vegetation. It is a low, flat plain, from 20 to 26 feet in altitude, broken only by a series of hills of a maximum height of 325 feet including Champotón, Campeche, Maxcanú and Tzuccacab. All this region is extremely dry. It possesses some lakes, of which the largest, Lake Bacalar, in the south-east of Quintana Roo, measures 31 miles long by 6 to 7½ miles wide, and three little mountain streams, the Champotón in the west, the Lagartos in the north, the Zelhá in the east. Water is mainly provided by large natural wells or *cenotes*, which measure up to 195 feet in diameter and result from the collapse of surface calcareous stratum, laying bare a continuous bed of subterranean water.

This subterranean water lies only 16 feet below the surface near the northern coast, but it becomes deeper as one moves southwards and goes down to a depth of 100 feet and more.

These few brief indications are enough to show that the countryside occupied by the Mayas has no geographic homogeneousness and offers climates varying from the high region of the Cordillera, where frosts are frequent, to the region of the Petén where the temperature can fall to 10° centigrade during the winter and rise to 40° in April and May, and finally the northern part of Yucatán, with its extreme dryness.

LINGUISTICS[1]

The Mayan peoples can be divided linguistically into six groups.

All the Mayan languages are closely related to each other and linked geographically over a continuous territory, with the exception of Wastek.

(a) The *Wastek* group comprises: *Wastek*, previously spoken in the plains and hills of the Tampico region, from the Rio Tuxpan to Sierra Tamaulipas and from the coast of the Gulf of Mexico to the

[1]*Les Langues du Monde* by a group of linguists under the direction of A. Meillet and Marcel Cohen. New edition. Paris 1952. (Names of extinct dialects are preceded by an asterisk.)

first valleys of the eastern Sierra Madre. The *Wasteks* are now reduced to less than 50,000 individuals, grouped in two quite limited zones, one in the south-east of the State of San Luis Potosí (Tancanhuitz and Cuidad Valles regions), the other in the north of the State of Vera Cruz (Tantoyuca, Chontla, Amatlan and Tancoco regions). Each of these two zones has a different dialect.

Cikomuseltek which formerly appears to have been called *Coxoh*, was still spoken at the beginning of the twentieth century in the village of Chicomucelo in the south of Chiapas, near the Guatemalan frontier, over 500 miles from the Tampico region. Despite this distance, it can still be considered a simple dialect of *Wastek*.

(b) The *Mayan* group consists of a single language: *Maya* proper, still spoken by over 300,000 people, nearly all grouped in the State of Yucatán and in the northern portion of the State of Campeche, in the north-west of the peninsula of Yucatán. These northern Maya call themselves by the name of *Masewal* and speak a fairly uniform tongue. This language is also found, with only very slight differences, in the more southern regions of the peninsula, where it would appear that it was planted by several groups of recent immigrants from the north. The first were the Itzá, natives of Chichén Itzá, who had been settled in Petén since the fifteenth century. Then the *Maya-Masewal* arrived, individually or in small groups, fleeing to the almost deserted southern forests to escape Spanish colonization; their descendants can be found to-day as far as Tenosique (Tabasco).

The real southern Mayan groups seem to have spoken dialects differing somewhat from the classical *Maya* of the north. Sixteenth-century documents cite *Mopan* and *Kehače*. *Mopan* dialect is still spoken by some hundreds of individuals on the frontier of Petén and British Honduras. It is very similar to *Čol* and more complete documentation might make it possible to class it as a *Čol* dialect. Practically nothing is known of the *Kehače* or *Masatek* Indians except that they were Maya and that they disappeared from the region they formerly occupied in the north of Petén. They might possibly have been driven southwards by the pressure of Maya escaping from Spanish Yucatán, and their present descendants may be the *Lakandón* of Chiapas (Fig. 6), who call themselves *Winik* and are sometimes wrongly called by the name of *Karib*. It is known that these *Lakandón* Indians have taken over the territory and name of an ancient *Čol* group, deported by the Spaniards. The present *Lakandón* speak a *Mayan* dialect.

(c) The Čol group comprises several languages which are related to those of the *Tseltal* group on the one hand, and have, on the other, quite close affinities with *Mopan* and *Maya* proper. It is thought that the peoples of this group formerly extended from Tabasco to Honduras. The disappearance of several tribes during the colonial period broke the old geographical continuity.

Tokegwa was spoken in the hills rising not far from the banks of the Gulf of Honduras, between the lower courses of the Rivers Motagua and Ulua. This language has not been described, but an eighteenth-century author (F. Ximenez) assures us that the *Tokegwa* belonged to the same nation as the Čols and the Čortis.

Čorti is still spoken by over 30,000 people on either side of the frontier separating Guatemala and Honduras, in the region of Copán, Yucatán, La Unión and Quetzaltepec. In the sixteenth century, it extended east towards the present town of Gracias, southwards to Chalatenango (Salvador), and northwards probably to the vicinity of Lake Izabal and the high valley of Chamelecon.

Čol was spoken, in a zone of tropical forests, by several tribes or local groups who for a long time resisted Spanish colonization and against whom rigorous measures were finally taken. The *Akala*, settled between the Río de la Pasión, and the *Manče*, who lived in the north of Lake Izabal, were deported to the *Kiče* region of Guatemala where they interbred and lost their language. Their former territory was occupied by the *Kekči* coming from the south. The Čol-Lakandón were settled on the middle course of the Usumacinta and, farther west, in the region of the Rivers Jataté, Lacanhá and Lacantún: they were transferred to Chiapas, and the present Čols —about 25,000 of them, almost all of whom live to the west of Palenque—would appear to be their descendants. The former territory of the Čol-Lakandón was invaded in the seventeenth and eighteenth centuries by Indians from the north who spoke a dialect of *Maya* proper and to whom the name of *Lakandón* was wrongly transferred. Amongst the present Cols of Chiapas, at least three dialects exist, which differ considerably from the *Manče* which an eighteenth-century vocabulary has preserved for us. *Palenkano*, a Čol dialect from Palenque, forms a sort of transition to Čontal.

The Čontal known as *Tabasco* is spoken by almost 20,000 people at the mouth of the Rivers Grijalva and Usumacinta. It formerly extended south-eastwards to Tenosique and north-eastwards to the regions of Acalán and Champotón. Two dialects of it still exist: one called *Yokotan*, spoken near the town of Macuspana, the other called

Čontal proper, spoken in Chontalpan, that is to say, in the delta of the Rio Grijalva. An ancient text has preserved a third dialect called **Wibat'an*, spoken in the sixteenth century in the region called Acalán, to the east and north-east of the Terminos lagoon. The name *Putun*, sometimes written *Puctun*, seems to have been employed by the ancient Maya to describe the *Čontal* and western *Čol* groups.

(*d*) *Tseltal* has affinities with the *Čol* group on one side and with the *Mam* group on the other. The languages of this group are as follows:

Tseltal is spoken by nearly 50,000 people in the centre of the State of Chiapas, around the town of Ocosingo and farther southwards, up to the Guatemalan frontier. *Bačaxon*, spoken in the north of Ocosingo, is a *Tseltal* dialect.

Tsotil or *Čamula* is spoken by over 60,000 people, also in the State of Chiapas but more to the west than *Tseltal*, notably around the towns of Simojoval and San Cristóbal.

Čañabal is spoken in Chiapas by tens of thousands of people living in the vicinity of Comitán or more to the south-west.

Čuxe has its principal centre in the town of San Mateo Ixtatan, to the north of Huehuetenango, in Western Guatemala. Spoken by about 15,000 people, it is very similar to *Čañabal* but in other respects shows close affinities with certain *Kanxobal* dialects.

(*e*) The *Mam* group comprises languages still insufficiently known. It would appear that the following dialects can be attributed to it:

Kanxobal, confused for a long time with *Čuxe*, was spoken to the south and east of the latter language, from San José Montenegro on the Mexican frontier to San Juan Ixcoy and Santa Cruz Barillas in Guatemala. It is divided into several dialects, including *Solomek*, spoken at San Pedro Soloma and *Xakaltek*, spoken at Jacaltenango and in the surrounding villages. The number of Indians speaking the *Kanxobal* tongue probably approaches 35,000–40,000.

Subinha, known only from an ancient document, was probably spoken in some villages of the *Kanxobal* region.

Motosintlak would have been spoken by 3,000 or 4,000 individuals grouped in a restricted area around the town of Motozintla, in the south of Chiapas, near the Guatemalan frontier.

Mam is spoken on either side of the southern Mexican-Guatemalan frontier, except on the coast. The present-day *Mams* probably number about 300,000 but most of them have succumbed to Spanish influence and ceased to use their indigenous language, especially in Chiapas. *Mam* would still be spoken by over 100,000 individuals, notably in the regions of Todos Santos, Cuchumatanes, Huehuetenango, San Marcos, Tajamulco, etc. This language comprises numerous dialects that have still only been slightly studied. Of these the last Mexican censuses mention *Koyotin*, *Takyal*, *Takaneko*, *Tutuapa*, *Takana*, and *Tlatiman*.

Agwakatek I is spoken by about 8,000 people in Guatemala. Its area is very restricted, being limited to the neighbourhood of the town of Aguacatan, to the east of Huehuetenango.

Ixil or *Isil* is spoken by over 20,000 individuals in the regions of Nebaj, Cotzal and Chajul, to the north-east of the *Mam* territory, between the land of Čuxe and Uspantek. Although *Ixil* has affinities with *Kiče*, it would seem rather to belong to the *Mam* sub-group.

(*f*) The *Kiče* group comprises the following dialects:

Kiče, which was once a powerful language and is still spoken over a vast territory of present-day Guatemala, to the west of Lake Atitlán and to the north of Rio Matagua, from Ratalhuleu and Mazatenango to Scapula and Rabinal. It also includes a small group in the south of Chiapas, not far from the town of Tapachula. The *Kiče* are at present the largest group of the Mayan people and number over 400,000 individuals.

Kakčikel is still spoken by nearly 350,000 people on the eastern and northern banks of Lake Atitlán and in a region more to the east, notably around the centres of Solola, Chimaltenango and Antigua.

Tsutuhil, spoken by tens of thousands of people in a small region situated on the southern banks of Lake Atitlán includes some variant dialects. In the pre-Columbian epoch the *Tsutuhil* had to withstand wars against the *Kiče* and *Kakčikel* and this probably helped to reduce their territory.

Uspantek is spoken by about 3,000 people in a restricted area with its centre at San Miguel Uspantan to the north of the *Kiče* country.

Kiče, *Kakčikel*, *Tsutuhil* and *Uspantek* are grouped in Guatemala in a very densely populated zone and are so closely connected that they can be considered straightforward dialects of the same language. In the sixteenth century, they were designated *en bloc* under the name of *Ači*. It is generally agreed that these languages formerly covered territory up to the Pacific coast; but, in actual fact, our information is deficient on the early linguistic state of this coastal region of Guatemala, where the density of population has always been low, where the *Nawa* (*Yuto-Astek* family) played a great role in the sixteenth century and where Spanish is nowadays used almost exclusively.

Kekci was spoken in the sixteenth century in a not particularly extensive region round the towns of Cahabon and Coban in Verapaz. Since this period, the *Kekči* have taken advantage of the deportation of the eastern *Čol* to assimilate the remainder of these people and have spread over considerable territory northwards and eastwards. They number at present nearly 250,000 and occupy the larger part of the department of Alta Verapaz. They can even be found in Petén, in the department of Izabal and in the south of British Honduras.

Pokomam was spoken in the sixteenth century from the region of Amatitlán, Guatemala and Mixco to the point where the present frontiers of Guatemala, Salvador and Honduras meet. More to the south-east, it survived in the *Nawa* zones (*Yuto-Astek*) in the isolated towns of Ahuachapan, Chalchuapan, San Salvador and Iztepeque. This suggests that, before the *Pipil* invasion, it was possibly the language of Western Salvador up to Rio Lampa. *Pokomam* has now entirely disappeared from Salvador but is still spoken in Guatemala by about 25,000 people, distributed in a few linguistic enclaves, notably in the neighbourhood of Antigua and Jalapa.

Pokomči is spoken by over 30,000 people, to the south of Coba, in the region of the sources of the Rio Cahabon. *Pokomči* barely differs from *Pokomam*. The two languages are sometimes collectively designated as *Pokom*. In the sixteenth century they were separated territorially by a group of *Pipil*, who came from Mexico and succumbed to Spanish influence in the colonial epoch.

Kekči, *Pokomam* and *Pokomči* have special affinities with each other which make it permissible to group them in one *Kekči-Pokom* section.

*   *   *

This study will not consider the *Wastek*, who lived and still live in the lowlands in the north of the State of Vera Cruz and in the foothills of the Sierra, in the east of the State of San Luis de Potosí. In actual fact, these Indians, although they undoubtedly speak a Mayan dialect and physically resemble their brothers from Yucatán, have a civilization which differs in essential points from that of the latter: they have never constructed buildings similar to those of Yucatán and Petén, and they have no knowledge of the

[1] BONAMPAK. J. Eric Thompson and a group of Lakandón Indians in front of the Palace of the Frescoes. (*Photo Giles G. Healey.*)

[2] PALENQUE. Hieroglyphics in stucco. (*Photo Henri Lehmann.*)

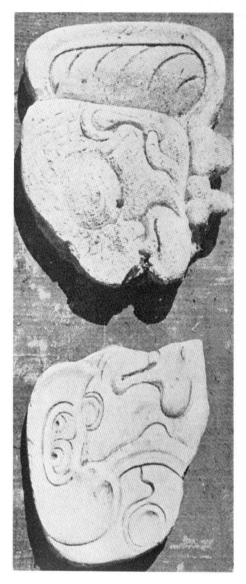

[3] PALENQUE. Hieroglyphics in stucco. (*Photo Henri Lehmann.*)

[4] Arch which marks the beginning of the Kabah–Uxmal road. (*Photo Alberto Ruz Lhuillier.*)

[5] LABNÁ. Relief of the God Chac. (*Photo Henri Lehmann.*)

[6] LEYDEN PLAQUE. A Jade Plaque found in the neighbourhood of Puerto-Barrios (Guatemala), but undoubtedly originating from Tikal, according to Morley. (Rijksmuseum voor Volkenkunde.)

[7] LABNÁ. The 'Mirador' with large 'Roof Comb'. (*Photo Henri Lehmann.*)

[8] COPÁN. Funeral Urn from the Archaeological Museum of Copán. (*Photo Jesús Núñez Chinchilla.*)

[9] LABNÁ. Mask of the God of Rain. (*Photo Alberto Ruz Lhuillier.*)

[10] PALENQUE. Central personage in the Panel of the Slaves. (*Photo Alberto Ruz Lhuillier.*)

[11] PALENQUE, Temple of the Sun. (Photo, Alberto Ruz Lhuillier.)

[12] KABAH. Detail of the Façade of the K'odzp'op. (*Photo Henri Lehmann.*)

[13] LABNÁ. (*Photo Henri Lehmann.*)

[14] LABNÁ. The Arch. (*Photo Henri Lehmann.*)

15 KABAH. Façade of the K'odzp'op with stylizations of the God Chac. (*PhotoHenri Lehmann.*)

6] KABAH. The
'odzp'op' (Petate
rollado). Mask of
e God of Rain.
hoto Alberto Ruz
uillier.)

7] LABNÁ. Mask
the God of Rain
the frieze of the
lace. (Photo Alberto
z Lhuillier.)

[18] CHICHÉN ITZÁ. Chased Gold Plate from the dredging of the Cenote of Sacrifices. (*After I. Marquina.* '*Arquitectura prehispánica*', p. 898.)

overhanging arch (cf. pp. 100–101). Isolated some 300 miles to the north-west, they are separated from the mass of the Mayan people by the Totonak and Nahuatl peoples from the centre and the south of the State of Vera Cruz.

All this can only be explained by a very early separation that preceded the formation of Mayan civilization, i.e. it must have taken place towards the end of the first millennium B.C.

PHYSICAL TYPE

The Maya (Fig. 1) were rather small, the average height of the men was 5 feet, and of the women 4 feet 7 inches. They had broad, short skulls; in other words, they are amongst the most brachycephalic peoples of the world. Indeed, the relationship between the width and length of their heads, that is to say, their cephalic index, rises to 85·8 with men and 86·8 with women. The head was only slightly developed in height. The nose was prominent, straight backed or sometimes slightly aquiline. The relationship between the height and the breadth of the nose, i.e. the nasal index, varies according to the series studied, from 45·28 to 49·05; it is particularly low and puts the Maya in the Leptorhine class of peoples. Their faces were broad and flat with prominent cheek-bones, and showed marked prognathism. The palpebral slope was sometimes slightly oblique and the eyes often showed the fold at the inner corner, so common amongst Asiatics. The skin was brownish or copper-coloured, the eyes dark brown or black. The hair was soft, black or very dark brown. Generally, no beard or moustache is found. However, in the codices, in the sculptures of the monuments or in the decoration of the pottery (Fig. 8), the artists quite often depict individuals with pointed beards and moustaches (Figs. 8, 115). The God Itzamná is often represented in this way.

Like all the American Indians the Maya very frequently bore a congenital pigmentary spot, wrongly called the Mongolian spot. It was a greenish colour and was located at the level of the sacral region. It rapidly disappeared with age.

The Maya had very definite physiological characteristics. Their blood belonged to Group O in the proportion of 97·7 per cent. Their basal metabolism was from 5 to 8 per cent higher than that of the North American man. The number of their pulsations was 52 per minute as compared with 72 for white men.

M.C.—C

II

HISTORY

THE Mayan civilization only entered history at the beginning of the Christian era. The peoples who were to be its inventors and propagators had occupied the hot lands around Petén for 3,000 years. They were nomad tribes who lived by hunting, fishing and casual food-gathering and for centuries knew nothing of agriculture, ceramics and architecture. In about 1000 B.C. their neighbours in the high lands of western Guatemala introduced them to maize,[1] the essential element of an agricultural civilization—and the technique of ceramics. Very probably these neighbours themselves spoke a Mayan dialect.

It was only at the beginning of the year 350 B.C. that the first architectural works in stone appeared in Petén, succeeding the wooden constructions. According to S. Morley, this architecture, characterized by the pseudo-corbelled vaulting (cf. p. 102), in conjunction with a particular hieroglyphic writing and a special chronological system, constituted Mayan civilization, properly speaking. The American scholar thinks that it is in Petén itself, at Tikal and Uaxactún, sites only 11 miles apart, that the first dated manifestations of this civilization are found. A jade plaque, originating from the Tikal region (Fig. 6) and preserved at the Museum of Leyden, goes back to A.D. 320, Stele 9 from Uaxactún to A.D. 328.

But Mexican archaeologists, led by Alfonso Caso, believe that earlier dates are given by remains originating from the south of the State of Vera Cruz in Mexico, and consequently locate the origin of Mayan civilization in the region corresponding to the centre of the Olnec civilization. A stele found at Tres Zapotes bears the date 21 B.C., and a jade figurine discovered at San Andres Tuxtla, A.D. 162. On the other hand, a stele from El Baul, in the

[1]Botanists are still not yet agreed on the exact origins of maize, some attributing the discovery of its cultivation to the populations of upper Peru, others to those of western Guatemala. The first base their argument on the abundant varieties of maize in the Peruvian Cordillera, the second on the existence in Guatemala of the only two plants which can be crossed with maize: teocintle (*Euchlaena mexicana* Schrader) and *Tripsacum L.*

high region of Guatemala, department of Escuintla—a completely different region—bears the date A.D. 41. Morley disputes the value of these three pieces of evidence either because they do not show Mayan characteristics, or because the very reading of the date appears doubtful to him.

Only time will decide this dispute between eminent archaeologists.

Whatever the answer, it is from A.D. 320, marked on the plaque at Leyden, that Americanists date the beginning of true Mayan history. The long period which preceded it, habitually called pre-Maya, might more correctly be termed prehistoric.

Mayan history has been divided into two periods: the period of the Old Empire, from 320 to 987, and the period of the New Empire, which extends from 987 to the Spanish conquest.

Naturally, the word 'empire' in these designations has no political meaning. It simply describes a homogeneous cultural ensemble, incorporating populations united by linguistic, artistic and social ties.

THE OLD EMPIRE

The Old Empire consists of three periods, the first covering three centuries (320–633), characterized by ceramics known as the Tzakol type (p. 205), the second only lasting for one century (633–731) during which the type of ceramics known as Tepeu (p. 205) appeared, and the third, lasting for two and a half centuries (731–987) saw both the maximum grandeur and the decadence of the Old Empire.

The most important Mayan ruins of the Old Empire are now related with certainty to each of these three periods. The following is an almost definitive table and chronology of these. When there are two dates in parentheses, the first indicates the oldest date of the site, the second the most recent.

First Period (320–633)

Tikal (320–867); Uaxactún (328–987); Balakbal (406); Uolantún (409); Copán (460–801); Oxkintok (475); Altar de Sacrificios (475); Xultún (475–889); Toniná (495–790); Chichén Itzá (495–1194); Yaxchilán (Menché) (514–761); Calakmul (514–810); Naachtún (524); Piedras Negras (534–810); Palenque (536–783); Tulum (564–1516); Ichpaatún (564); Pusilhá (573); Yaxhá (end of sixth.

century); La Honradez; Cobá (609–732); Uxul (613–810); Natanjo (615–810); Tzibanché (618–909); Chinkultic (628–810); El Encanto (first half of seventh century).

Second Period (633–731)

El Tortuguero (645); Jainá (652); El Amparo (655); Etzná (672–810); Tilá (685–830); Bonampak (692); Tzendales (692); Lacanhá (692); Quexil (692); Quiriguá (692–810); Chakanputún (692–948); El Palmar (711); Itsimté (721); Xamantún (La Mueñca) (721–889); La Florida (731); Oxpemul (731–830).

Third Period (731–987)

Santa Rosa Xtampak (751); Holactún (Xcalumkin) (764); Nakúm (771–849); Polol (790); Cancuén (790); Aguas calientes (790); Santa Elena Poco Uinic (790); Tayasal (790–867); Seibal (790–867); Ixkún (790–859); La Milpa; Tzimin Kax (810); La La Amelia (810); El Cayo; El Caribe; La Mar; Ucanal (849); Benque Viejo (849); Ixlú (859–870); Quen Santo (879); Los Higos (Honduras).

Right from the beginning of the Old Empire, the Maya adopted the practice of erecting steles or monuments at the end of each period of twenty years or *katún* (to be precise 19 years 7 months), then soon at the end of each half-*katún* (ten years or, more precisely, 9 years 8 months), and finally, exceptionally, at the end of each quarter of a *katún*, i.e. every five years (or more exactly 4 years 9 months). It is these dated steles that have made it possible to reconstruct the history of the Old Empire.

Between 337 and 435, Mayan civilization remained restricted to a radius of some thirty miles around Tikal and Uaxactún, with centres at Balakbal and Uolantún. But after 435, Mayan expansion developed great impetus. Within a century, monuments were erected at Oxkintok, Altar de Sacrificios, Toniná, Xultún, Piedras Negras, Yaxchilán, Palenque, Calakmul and Naachtún.

The expansion was primarily westwards (Palenque and Toniná), but also reached north-west Yucatán (Oxkintok and Chichén Itzá which the Itzá discovered in 485 and occupied in 514) on the one hand, and Copán in the south, on the other.

From 534 to 633, the Maya founded ten new cities, half of which were situated in the very centre of their domain, one (Chinkultic) in the high lands of the south-west, and four (Tzibanché, Ichpaatún, Tulum and Cobá) in the eastern region of Yucatán hitherto not reached.

During the second period of the Old Empire, which only lasted for a century, fourteen new centres were established, marking a slight advance westwards (El Tortuguero and Tilá), an infiltration towards the north (Oxpemul, Xamantún) and towards the western coast of Yucatán (Etzná and Jainá) and finally towards the south (Quiriguá). It was at the end of this period (692) that the Itzá abandoned Chichén to settle in Chakanputún on the Río Champotón.

The third period of the Old Empire is distinguished by a magnificent artistic upsurge followed by rapid and almost total decadence. Between 731 and 790 the Maya constructed three great new centres in Petén and Chiapas, Nakúm, Bonampak and Seibal, and many secondary centres, with extension westwards (Santa Elena Poco Uinic), southwards (Cancuén, Los Higos), south-eastwards (Exkún) and towards the extreme north (Santa Rosa Xtampak and Holactún). The year 790 marks the date of the maximum expansion of the Old Empire.

Decadence set in after 850, when only three centres erected monuments marking the end of Katún 19: Uaxactún and Oxpemul in the central zone and Tilá in Chiapas.

In 849, the number of sites where commemorative monoliths were erected was again five: it fell to two in 859, to three in 867, to four in 879, to three in 889. The last date of the Old Empire so far discovered is on a jade pendant originating from Tzibanché. It corresponds to the year 909.

The decline and disappearance of the dated monument evidently did not mark the end of the Mayan centres of the Old Empire. Urban life must have persisted in many of these centres but at gradually decreasing rhythm. This cultural collapse remains a mysterious phenomenon. The most diverse hypotheses have been put forward to explain it: earth tremors, climatic changes, epidemics, external or civil wars, exhaustion of the soil. Many of these hypotheses must be rejected.

It does not appear that the Mayan country suffered particularly from serious seismic disturbances or from a change of climate on a scale sufficient to enforce extensive migration.

On the other hand, the present state of knowledge does not seem to show that malaria or yellow fever existed in America before the European conquest. A foreign invasion would have left traces that archaeology has not so far found. As for the hypothesis of civil war so serious as to cause the abandonment of a territory as vast as the Old Mayan Empire, it scarcely seems acceptable.

In short, it seems that the cause of the eclipse of the ancient Maya must be sought in the exhaustion of the tropical soil as a result of inappropriate techniques of cultivation. It is now known that tropical soils do not have the fertility of temperate countries. A hectare of rice fields in the Tonkin delta produces 3,300 lb. of rice, whereas in the Po Valley the harvest is 13,200 lb. Tropical soils are also exhausted more rapidly than the soils of temperate regions. This explains the nomadism of the Indian tribes of the Amazon, for example. But the ancient Maya, like many primitive peoples, practised the disastrous system of cultivation known by the Indo-Chinese term *ray*, which is also rife in Madagascar, Africa, South America, etc. The forest is cut down and burnt at the end of the dry season and the seeds are sown in the ashes at the beginning of the rainy season. At the end of three years, the yield from the culti-vated land has diminished so much that the cultivator is obliged to transfer himself elsewhere. In our own time, certain Jewish colonies in Paraguay have had to give up an agricultural life be-cause of the impoverishment of the soil caused by too intensive exploitation and have had to seek new occupations in the urban centres to provide for their needs. An analogous factor must have obliged the ancient Maya to abandon their first territories. It can also not be excluded that this impoverishment of the soil brought with it the progressive under-nourishment of the cultivator and, as a result, his susceptibility to disease. What is certain is that at the end of the tenth century, all the towns of the Old Empire had been abandoned.

THE NEW EMPIRE

It has already been pointed out that the incursions from the territories of the Old Empire had penetrated to the northern part of Yucatán. Tzibanché, Ichpaatún, Tulum, Cobá, Chichén Itzá, Oxkintok were founded in this way in the first period of the Old Empire, Etzná and Jainá during the second, Santa Rosa Xtampak and Holactún during the third. The discovery and occupation of Chichén by the Itzá in 495 has also been mentioned and their abandonment of the town in 692 to occupy Chakanputún; they returned there in 879 and finally reoccupied it in 987.

The ten dated cities just enumerated fall into two groups, re-sulting from two migratory currents. One followed the eastern coast of Yucatán (Tzibanché, Ichpaatún, Tulum, Cobá and Chichén

Itzá) and the other, the western coast (Santa Rosa Xtampak, Etzná, Holactún, Jainá, Oxkintok).

It was in the north of Yucatán that the New Mayan Empire (p. 10) flourished. It covered a period, known as the Puuc period, or the period of the Mayan Renaissance or the League of Mayapán (987–1194), a Mexican period or the period of the hegemony of Mayapán (1194–1441), and finally a period of disintegration which lasted for a century (1441–1546) and came to an end with the Spanish conquest of the Maya.

The main agent of the Mayan renaissance was a migration of Maya-speaking peoples settled for two or two and a half centuries in the south-west of the present State of Campeche, in the vicinity of Chakanputún. They were partly Itzá, partly Indians from the central Mexican plateau, commanded by Kukulkán. About 928–948 these Indians began to move towards the north-west and settled at Chichén Itzá in 987. In the same year Kukulkán founded the town of Mayapán; a family by the name of Cocom was placed at the head. Uxmal was then founded in 1007 by a *cacique* called Ah Zuitok Titul Xiú, from the south-west, undoubtedly, like Kukulkán, of Mexican origin and more precisely from the Toltec region of Tula. The Mexican origin of the two chiefs by no means led to the introduction of their language into Yucatán. Both of them, like their subjects, had adopted the Mayan language during their long sojourn in the region of Chakanputún. But the adoption of the Mayan language did not mean that Mexican traditions were forgotten, and it is thus that, at Chichén Itzá as at Mayapán, Mexican cultural influence is evident.

Between 987 and 1007, the chiefs of the three towns formed an alliance, called the League of Mayapán. This was an extraordinarily brilliant epoch, when the artisans constructed the admirable monuments of Chichén Itzá and Uxmal and the new centres of Kabah (Figs. 12, 15, 16), Labná (Figs. 5, 7, 9, 13, 14, 17, 21, 22), Sayil and Izamal. A civil war between Chichén Itzá and Mayapán was to put an end to this magnificent upsurge. It appears that this fratricidal battle had been engendered by political and economic rivalry between the two regions, between the Cocomes of Mayapán, led by Hunac Ceal, and the Itzá of Chichén; the latter were finally driven from their town in 1194, and their *cacique* and the principal chiefs shut up at Mayapán as hostages. Mexican mercenary troops from the region west of the Terminos Lagoon, in the eastern part of the State of Tabasco, intervened in the war as auxiliaries of the Cocomes, and as supporters of the domination of the latter after victory.

The tyranny of Mayapán gradually became so intolerable that in 1441 a revolt took place; Mayapán was sacked and the chief of the town massacred. The captive chiefs, freed by the uprising, retired to their respective provinces, and all centralized authority disappeared from the north of Yucatán. The Empire disintegrated into a score of small provinces, continually struggling against each other, while the large urban centres became depopulated. This period of disintegration (1441–1546) was marked by a hurricane in 1464 and by serious epidemics in 1480, and 1515 or 1516. The second epidemic was smallpox, definitely brought by the first Spaniards who landed at Yucatán in 1511.

After the fall of Mayapán, the Itzá chief of Chichén Itzá retired with his people to the banks of Lake Petén, where in 1441 he re-occupied Tayasal, abandoned since the second half of the ninth century; a noble family from Mayapán, the Cheles, settled at Tecoh.

The sole surviving son of the assassinated Cocom chief of Mayapán led the rest of his subjects from Mayapán to Tibolón, near Sotuta. The Tutul Xiues did not return to Uxmal and founded the capital of Mani.

Broken up, dislocated, the Mayan people could not offer effective resistance to the white invader. However, the Spaniards, who had set foot in Yucatán in 1511, only completed the Indian conquest in 1697, the date when Martín de Ursáa seized Tayasal, the last stronghold of Itzá resistance.

III

LIFE AND BELIEFS

MATERIAL LIFE

THE Mayan house was sometimes built on a platform, as at Uaxactún, and resembled those still in use at the present time.

The plan of the dwelling was either rectangular or square. Sometimes the small sides were rounded and the four angles had the corners cut off. The rectangular seems to be the original form. However, huts of circular shape were not unknown and are still used by certain Mayan tribes in the State of Chiapas.

For details of construction, archaeologists have been reduced to using records shown in bas-reliefs (Figs. 22, 77), frescoes, graffiti, and the codices. These records show that the old Mayan house resembled the modern dwelling.

The material used to construct the walls varied with the resources of the region: stone in the north of Yucatán, rough bricks dried in the sun in Guatemala, wood or vegetable materials in the south of Yucatán. The house would measure from 21 feet 9 inches to 23 feet 9 inches long, by 11 feet 9 inches to 13 feet 9 inches wide. The walls were made of posts covered with mud or uncut stones 8 feet high. This base was continued by a wooden wall rising to 11 feet 6 inches or 14 feet 9 inches, supporting a roof with two very steep slopes, covered with palm leaves.

In the more comfortable houses, the interior was divided lengthwise by a partition covered with stucco and sometimes with paintings. The entrance room was the living and reception room; the back room was the bedroom. Small wooden chairs and probably hammocks, low tables and mats furnished the entrance room. The bedroom contained beds made of wooden frames covered with rush mats. Cotton covers were used during the cold season.

Male clothing comprised a cotton band about the width of a hand which went round the waist and passed between the thighs to cover the sexual organs. The two ends of this band were decorated to a greater or lesser degree, and fell respectively on the buttocks and on the lower part of the stomach. The men also wore a covering

41

called *pati* which covered the shoulders, and deerskin sandals fastened to the foot by cords made of Mexican fibre.

The men wore their hair long but with a wide tonsure at the top of their heads. They gathered their hair in long plaits wound round the skull and arranged in a pigtail which fell on to the nape of the neck and a sort of frontal fringe held in place by a band made of cotton or bark material.

The nobles wore the same garments as the common man, but enriched by various ornaments: feather headdresses, jade jewels at the breast, and belt and sandals decorated with jade, armlets and leg-guards. The most popular headwear consisted of feathers from the quetzal (*Trogon pavoninus* Hern) imported from Upper Guatemala where this sacred bird lives. The nobles were also distinguished by ornaments in their noses, ears and lips.

The priests wore long cloaks reaching to their ankles, either of cotton or of tree-bark made into material by a process of hammering.

The female garment consisted of a wide, long skirt open at the sides and tight at the waist. The women from the coast and from the province of Bacalar and Campeche also wore a piece of material or *pati*, the top edge of which went under the armpits and covered the top part of the body. All Indian women covered their heads with white cotton mantles. They painted themselves from the top of their bodies down to the waist, except for the breasts. They had long hair gathered in two or four plaits, with fringes similar to the men's on their foreheads. The little girls arranged their hair in the form of two or four horns. The noble women wore ornaments in their ears.

The ornaments of the common people were limited to nose rings, labrets and ear-rings made of bone, wood, shell and stone.

Men and women used stamps of engraved pottery soaked in colour to paint their bodies.

The young people, up to the time of marriage, painted their faces and bodies in black; after marriage they adopted red as their colour, only reverting to black at the times of the fasts.

The warriors painted themselves in red and black, the slaves in black with white stripes. Blue was reserved for priests, and associated with religious ceremonies, in particular those of the month of *mol*, on which occasion the instruments of the priests, the spindle wheels of the women and the posts of the dwellings were coated with this colour. At the end of the New Empire, it was associated with the idea of human sacrifice.

The Indians tattooed their bodies as well as painting them.

Apart from cranial deformation, the two sexes practised dental

PLATE II—BONAMPAK. ROOM 1. Frescoes from the southern wall. Below, the first personage from the string of musicians on the eastern wall and three personages who have unfortunately badly suffered, separated by bands of hieroglyphics; above, a group of important personages, continuing the similar group of the eastern wall with, at the extreme right, a platform on which an individual is standing holding a child in his arms, its head enclosed in the device used for artificial deformation. (Carnegie Institution of Washington, Department of Archaeology. Photo by Giles G. Healey, from reproductions by Antonio Tejeda.)

mutilation: cutting the incisors or encrusting them with small circular blocks of iron pyrites, obsidian or, more rarely, jade.

Daily life followed a regular rhythm. The day began in the early morning. Fire was obtained by the rapid gyratory movement of a pointed stick of hard wood in cavities hollowed out in a piece of soft wood. The women, who got up at about three or four o'clock, prepared a breakfast composed of maize tortillas and beans, and of nothing but *atole* in the poorest families. *Atole* is a hot drink obtained by dissolving a paste of maize in water, boiling it, and sweetening it with honey.

The preparation of food then occupied the greatest part of the woman's day. First of all she had to shell the maize, then cook it in a pot on the fireplace made of three stones. This had to be done in such a way that the maize could easily be removed from its covering. Finally, she had to grind it on a flat stone called a *caa*, with the help of a stone roller or *kab*.

An hour before the principal meal, the woman flattened (on a banana leaf) a bit of maize paste or *zacán* the size of an egg, made it into a round tortilla, placed it on a clay disk called a *xamach*, fitted on the fireplace. Once the tortillas are cooked they are shut in a calabash to keep hot.

Another maize preparation is called *pozole*. It is very similar to *zacán*, and is kept wrapped up in a banana leaf. It is mainly eaten outside the house, at the place of work, after being dissolved in a pitcher of water.

The principal meal, which was eaten one hour before sunset, comprised hot maize tortillas, beans, eggs, a little meat, vegetables and chocolate, depending on the resources of the family.

Chocolate was manufactured from cocoa-beans, roasted and ground and boiled with powdered maize and pimento.

After eating, the man took his daily hot bath in a wooden basin hollowed in a cedar trunk.

The night meal was light and similar to morning breakfast.

The family went to bed at eight or nine o'clock.

Male occupations were primarily agricultural and consisted essentially of the cultivation of maize. To prepare a field the Maya had first to cut down the trees of the forest—a long and hard operation for men who only possessed stone tools. He then had to set fire to these trees and to the underwood, and finally to sow the seeds in the ashes of the fire. Because of the rapid exhaustion of the ground, as has already been emphasized, new fields had to be prepared every four or five years.

The Maya joined together in groups of sixteen to twenty to perform the hardest agricultural tasks. These collective parties were principally for cutting down the forest to create new centres of cultivation. The night preceding the work was a night of festivity; before beginning the task, prayers were addressed and offerings of *copal* made to the gods of the earth.

The trees were cut down in the very middle of the rainy season, in August, the fire made in March or April. These acts, as all those of Indian life, were accompanied by religious practices. The day was chosen by the priests. Sowing commenced immediately after the first rains, during the month of May. Five or six seeds were placed in holes $3\frac{1}{2}$–5 inches deep, made with a pointed stick, spaced at intervals of 4 feet, then the holes were closed by foot. The sower observed continence during the operation.

Between May and September, the cultivator had to weed his field once or more until the harvest. This was done by hand.

Once the maize was ripe, in September or October, each stem was bent towards the soil, at the base of the ear. A month later— that is, in November—the harvest began and lasted till March or April. But it was at its height in January–February.

The maize was kept in the ear, after it had been removed from its external covering or after shelling, and was stored either in granaries on the field itself or in receptacles in the houses.

Apart from maize and cocoa, the Maya cultivated beans (*búul*), (*Phaseolus vulgaris* L.), calabash (*Crescentia Cujete*, L.), sweet potato (*Ipomea Batatas* Poir), tomato (*Lycopersicum esculentum* Mill.), manioc (*Manihot utilissima* Phol.), chayote or guisquil (*Sechium edule* Sw.), chaya (*Jatropha urens* L.), jicama (*Jatropha macrorhiza* Benth.), mamey (*Lucuma mammosa* Gaertn.), avocado pear (*Persea gratissima* Gaertn.), chico-zapote (*Achras Sabota* L.), papaw (*Carica Papaya* L.), anona (*Anona muricata* L.), maranon (*Anacardium occidentale* L.), guayaba (*Psidium Guayava* Raddi.), siricote (*Cordia dodecandra*), nance (*Malpighia punicifolia* L.), ramon (*ox*) (*Brosimum alicastrum* Sw.), pimento (*Capsicum* L.), epazote (*Chenopodium ambrosioides*), culantro (*Coriandrum* L.).

They cultivated cotton, and used henequen and sisal fibres to make rope, and the fibre of the bayal palm tree to make baskets.

Mayan diet also depended on hunting. The stag, the peccary and the coati were hunted with dogs, or by using traps or snares. Bows and arrows did not appear until the Mexican period of the New Empire. Birds were hunted with blow-pipes using little pellets of hardened clay as projectiles; the Maya were not familiar with the use of the poisoned arrow. They had two species of domestic dog: one was a type of hound, used for hunting and as a watchdog, the other a hairless dog that did not bark and which was bred and fattened for consumption.

They had also domesticated the turkey, the ara and a type of bee without sting,[1] which they kept near their houses in hives consisting of wooden cylinders closed at the extremity by stones and clay and having an opening for flight. Honey was used particularly in the manufacture of a fermented drink called *balche*.

The Maya constructed roads (*saché*) with the local calcareous stone; they were causeways raised 2–8 feet. Like the Inca roads they were rectilinear. The sides of the base were made of rough-hewn blocks; the roadway, 14 feet 6 inches wide, was covered with calcareous gravel which formed a sort of cement, hardening under the action of the humidity and the pressure exerted by stone rollers. One of these rollers, found at Ekal on the Cobá–Yaxuná causeway was 13 feet wide, 2 feet in diameter and weighed 5 tons. Some fifteen labourers were needed to move it. Apart from this Cobá–Yaxuná causeway, there was another which joined Kabah to Uxmal, the beginning of which was marked by a great arch (Fig. 4).

The Maya from the coastal region had large open boats capable of carrying forty men, and, in the region of Bakhalal, used double canoes provided with a sail and a crew of fourteen. A fresco from the Temple of the Warriors at Chichén Itzá depicts three short boats, the stern and prow of which are strongly and equally raised, with a rower standing at one end and two passengers also standing.

The festival of the fishermen was celebrated at the same time as that of the hunters during the month of *Zip*.

POLITICAL ORGANIZATION

As I have said already, the word Empire applied to the Mayan grouping gives an incorrect idea of its political organization. The only form of government in pre-Columbian America corresponding to the centralized conception of power expressed by the word 'empire', was that of the Incas. As Morley has very rightly remarked, the political bond of the Mayan people, united in a profound cultural, linguistic and religious community, resembled that

[1]Nordenskiöld, Erland, *L'Apiculture indienne*. Journal de la Société des Americanistes de Paris. Paris, new Series, vol. XXI, 1929, pp. 169–82.

of the ancient Greek cities: Sparta, Athens and Corinth between the sixth and second centuries B.C.; the Italian cities: Venice, Genoa and Florence between the eighth and fifteenth centuries, or the Hanseatic cities: Lübeck, Hamburg and Bremen, at roughly the same period. Each Mayan town was independent and had its own government and could contract alliances with the neighbouring towns to form confederations analogous to that exemplified in the New Empire with the League of Mayapán. Morley assumes that several arrangements of this nature must have existed during the Old Empire. The first, with Tikal as capital, comprising the centre and north of Petén in Guatemala, the south of Campeche in Mexico and British Honduras; a second comprising the valley of the Usumacinta, the centre of which might have been Palenque, Piedras Negras or Yaxchilán; a third in the south-east around Copán; and finally a grouping in the south-west around Toniná.

A chief called *Halach uinic* sat at the head of each of these city-states. His functions were hereditary and passed from father to eldest son, regency being exercised by the paternal uncles if the heir was a minor. It was he who decided on the external and internal politics of State with the help and advice of a council consisting of the principal chiefs, priests and important personages. It was he too who appointed the chiefs of the secondary centres and villages. Certain authors think that, apart from his civil power, he also exercised religious authority. The emblem of political power was an unusual sceptre held in the right hand, a round shield in the left. The religious emblem was an ornament that could be compared to a bit, the branches of which were decorated with two human heads and which was carried athwart the breast.

A war chief, *nacom*, elected for three years, commanded all the forces from the different centres of the State in case of conflict.

The army was a form of permanent militia. In peace-time the soldiers followed their occupations and lived in their houses like other members of the community. Only in case of war did they receive a small amount in pay. The conflict over, they returned to their villages and resumed normal life. This system, not unlike the Swiss system, is an obvious mark of the pacific character of the Mayan people—certainly one of the conditions of the rise of their magnificent civilization.

Offensive arms consisted of the spear, swords made of hard wood, about one yard long, their edges decorated with strips of obsidian, slings and boomerangs. Bows and arrows and the spear-thrower were introduced from Mexico during the New Empire.

The shield which, during the Old Empire, was square or round in shape, covered with jaguar or deer skin, was used for defence. During the New Empire, long and flexible shields appeared, undoubtedly made of plaited rushes.

Mayan society was divided into four classes: the nobles, the priests, the men of the people, and the slaves.

The nobility comprised the local chiefs of the centres dependent on the capital. These chiefs with the help of a local council of two or three persons exercised executive, administrative and judicial power in their centre and commanded a troop of soldiers. Their own subsistence was assured by their subjects, but they also collected the tribute money reserved for the *halach uinic*.

Justice was administered by the chief of the community to which the culprit belonged. The most severe punishment was slavery. The usual punishment consisted of fines to be paid in cotton coverings or cocoa beans.

Religious power seems, like civil power, to have been hereditary. The priests were not only responsible for religious ritual, the ceremonies of sacrifice and divination, but they were also remarkable astronomers and mathematicians. At the side of the priests were soothsayers or *chilanes*, sacrificers, who tore out the hearts of human victims, assistants or servants charged with accomplishing the material part of the rites. It would seem that the priests occupied a predominant place in Mayan society and were more influential than the nobility.

The people consisted of humble tillers who had to provide food for the chiefs and priests, participate in the construction of the great buildings, extracting and working the stones, cutting down the forests, sculpting the wood—artists, artisans and beasts of burden at one and the same time. Tribute money and offerings to the gods were a heavy burden to them. All these agricultural workers lived grouped in little villages, comprising but a few families, dispersed in the forest near the cultivated fields. The large centres, whose ruins have been explored by the archaeologists and which are called cities, were of an exclusively religious nature and were only inhabited by the most important priests and the civil chiefs.

The slaves or *ppentacoob* were recruited primarily from prisoners-of-war, but also from orphans and criminals in common law. They were indeed virtually bought and sold.

The merchants, grouped in corporations, formed a class apart. They had a fan as their insignia. They often made journeys lasting several months. Their protector god was the god of cocoa—its bean

[19] COPÁN. Mask of Venus, above and in the centre of the Stairway of the Jaguars. (*Photo Jesús Núñez Chinchilla.*)

[20] PALENQUE. El Palacio. Eastern Courtyard (eastern side). (*Photo Jacques Soustelle.*)

[21] LABNÁ. Sculptured head of the God Chac. (*Photo Henri Lehmann.*)

[22] LABNÁ. The Arch. Above the lateral doors, stylized cabins. (*Photo Henri Lehmann.*)

[23] PALENQUE. Hieroglyphic stairway of the principal courtyard of the palace. Building C. (*Photo Henri Lehmann.*)

[25] COPÁN. Temple 22. Sculptured head from the lower part of the framework of the door. (*Photo Joaquin Múñoz.*)

[24] COPÁN. Jaguar at the southern extremity of the Stairway of the Jaguars, Eastern Court. (*Photo Joaquin Múñoz.*)

[26] COPÁN. Temple 22. Sculpture from the framework of the door.
(*Photo François Chevalier.*)

[27] COPÁN. Spectators' Gallery, western end, Western Court. (*Photo Joaquin Múñoz.*)

COPÁN. Large sculpture at the west town and of the Sate At the Cont. West. G. A. AC L. 1891

[29] COPÁN. Spectators' Gallery. Profile of the head of the personage in Fig. 28. (*Photo François Chevalier.*)

[30] COPÁN. Stairway of the Hieroglyphics and Stele M with its altar. (*Photo Joaquin Múñoz.*)

[31] COPÁN. Sculpture from the north-eastern extremity of Temple II, known as 'The Old Man of Copán'. (*Photo Jesús Núñez Chinchilla.*)

[32] COPÁN. General view of the Ball Court. In the background Stele No. 2. (*Photo Joaquin Múñoz.*)

[34]

[33] COPÁN. Stele No. 5. (*Photo Jesús Núñez Chinchilla.*)

[34] COPÁN. Sculpture from the framework of the door, Temple 22. (*Photo Jesús Núñez Chinchilla.*)

[35] COPÁN. Stele B,
southern side. Principal
Court. (*Photo Joaquin
Múñoz.*)

66] COPÁN. Stele B, eastern side. Principal Court. (*Photo Musée de Homme.*)

[37] COPÁN. Stele H, western side. (*Photo Musée de l'Homme.*)

constituting an international currency. *Xamán Ek*, the Pole Star, was also worshipped by the merchants, who offered it copal at altars placed at the roadside.

These merchants exported cloaks of embroidered cotton, jade jewellery, etc. There was also internal trade in merchandise such as salt, marine shells, and cocoa.

WRITING

Evidence of Mayan writing is found both in manuscripts and in numerous inscriptions on bas-reliefs.

The manuscripts or *codices* were written on paper (*huun*). This was made from the fibres of a tree called *copó*, which is *Ficus cotinifolia*, impregnated with natural vegetable gum and covered with a layer of fine white lime, mixed or coated with starch.[1] The manuscripts were placed in a long band with the different parts or pages folded together like the shutters of a draught screen. Only three of these have survived: the *Codex dresdensis*, which is the oldest—possibly earlier than the tenth century A.D.; the *Codex peresianus*, which is owned by the Bibliothèque Nationale in Paris; and the *Codex Tro-cortesianus*, made up of two parts which have long since been shown to constitute a whole: the *Codex Troano* of the Library de Juan de Tro y Ortolano at Madrid and the *Cortesianus* from the Biblioteca del Palacio at Madrid.

The *Codex dresdensis* was found in Vienna in Austria and bought by the director of the Library of Dresden. The *Codex peresianus* was discovered in 1860 at the Bibliothèque Nationale in Paris, in a basket of old papers abandoned in a grate. The paper enclosing it bore the name of 'Perez' which was used to baptize it. The *Codex Tro-cortesianus* was found in Spain between 1860 and 1870, in two separate pieces. The two pieces are now united in the Museum of Archaeology and History at Madrid. This Codex is 23 feet 3 inches long, and consists of fifty-six leaves of 112 pages $9\frac{1}{2}$ inches high and 5 inches wide. The *Codex dresdensis* is 11 feet 4 inches long and has thirty-nine leaves or seventy-eight pages (of which four are blank), 10 inches high by $3\frac{1}{2}$ inches wide. The *Codex peresianus*, which is very fragmentary, is 4 feet 8 inches long and only consists of eleven leaves or twenty-two pages.

[1] Wolfgang von Hagen, Victor, *La Fabricación del papel entre los Aztecas y los Mayas*, Mexico, 1945.

M.C.—E

The *Codex dresdensis* is primarily an astronomical treatise, the *Codex Tro-cortesianus* a text of divination used by the priest to predict the future, and the *Codex peresianus* is essentially ritualistic.

The writing on the Mayan monuments consists of the painted or engraved inscriptions decorating the walls and steles of their religious buildings, the engraved inscriptions being by far the more numerous and the best preserved.

A remarkable group of investigators set their skill to work on this collection of documents. Their studies resulted in the deciphering of Mayan hieroglyphics and signs and thus in the understanding of Mayan mathematics and astronomy.

To write numbers the Maya used dots and horizontal lines. The dot was equivalent to one unit, the line to five units. For example, three super-posed lines, surmounted by four dots in a line, represented the number 19.

Their numbering was vigesimal whereas ours is decimal. Also, while our numbers are written horizontally and one number placed immediately to the left of another represents a unit ten times larger than the latter, Mayan numbers were written vertically one on top of the other, from bottom to top, and each number written immediately above another represented a unit twenty times larger than the latter. A number was therefore formed of super-posed signs corresponding to units, which numbering from bottom upwards, we will call units of the first order, second order, third order, etc.

Like us, the Maya knew zero, which they represented by a stylized shell.

Thus, the number 20 was represented by a shell surmounted by a dot, which signified that there were no first order units and one second unit, i.e. 20. To write 37, three lines surmounted by two order dots are needed, i.e. 17 first order units and one dot above, which indicated one second order unit, or 20; $17+20=37$; the number 300 was expressed by the sign for 0, indicating the absence of a first order unit, surmounted by three bars, that is, 15 second order units, thus 15×20 or 300. The number 7,113 was formed of the number 13 at the first order stage, the number 15 at the second order stage, or 15×20, or 300; the number 17 at the third order stage, i.e. $17 \times 20 \times 20 = 6,800$. The total makes 7,113.

The number 9,631 was formed of the number 11 at the first order stage, the number 1 at the second order stage, i.e. 1×20 or 20; the number 4 at the third order stage, i.e. $4 \times 400 = 1,600$, the number 1 at the fourth order stage, i.e. $1 \times 8,000$ or 8,000; the total $11+20+1,600+8,000=9,631$.

The number 181,613 comprised from bottom to top: the number 13 at the first order stage, the number 0 at the second order stage, the number 14 at the third order stage: $14 \times 400 = 5,600$; the number 2 at the fourth order stage: $2 \times 8,000 = 16,000$, the number 1 at the fifth order stage: $1 \times 160,000 = 160,000$, and $13 + 0 + 5,600 + 16,000 + 160,000 = 181,613$.

Apart from the system of transcribing numbers by lines and dots, the Maya represented numbers from 0 to 19 by glyphs each consisting of a head.

The writing also included twenty glyphs to designate each of the days of the religious calendar, nineteen glyphs to designate each of the months and the supplementary period of five days of the solar calendar, nine glyphs to designate each of the periods of time: *kin, uinal, tun, katún, baktún, piktún, kalabtún, kinchultún, alautún*; one glyph represented the moon, one glyph the planet Venus, four glyphs the cardinal points and the corresponding colours, nine glyphs the divinities of the nether world. The principal gods of the Maya Pantheon also had their glyphs. By now 150 hieroglyphics have been deciphered, nearly a third of the signs hitherto catalogued. The task of the archaeologists is yet further complicated by the fact that each glyph presents several variations.

Mayan writing was undoubtedly ideographic in essence but it would appear that it comprised certain syllabic elements. Its use was not completely abandoned until the beginning of the eighteenth century after the Spaniards had destroyed the last independent Mayan city, Tayasal in 1697. It can be stated with complete certainty that the Mayan hieroglyphic system is not connected in any way with the Egyptian system of hieroglyphics.

CHRONOLOGY

The unit of time of the Maya was the day or *kin*; twenty days constituted a month or *uinal*; they had the following names: *imix, ik, akbal, kan, chicchan, cimi, manik, lamat, muluc, oc, chuen, eb, ben, ix, men, cib, caban, exnab, canac, ahau.*

The names of the eighteen months or *uinal* were: *pop, uo, zip, zotz, tzec, xul, yaxkin, mol, chen, yax, zac, ceh, mac, kankin, muan, pax, kayab, cumhu.*

The days within each *uinal* were numbered from 0 to 19. For example, the Maya wrote 0 *pop*, 1 *pop*, 2 *pop* exactly as we write: February 1, February 2, etc.

Besides the day, and the month of twenty days, the Maya distinguished the following periods:

The *tun* which was 18 *uinal* or 360 days;
the *katún* which equalled 20 *tun* or 7,200 days;
the *baktún* which equalled 20 *katún* or 144,000 days;
the *piktún* which equalled 20 *baktún* or 2,880,000 days;
the *kalabtún* which equalled 20 *piktún* or 57,600,000 days;
the *kinchiltún* which equalled 20 *kalabtún* or 1,52,000,000 days;
the *alautún* which equalled 20 *kinchiltún* or 23,040,000,000 days.

Chronology, like enumeration, was therefore on a vigesimal basis, with the exception of the *tun*. This arose from the fact that the Maya sought to harmonize their calendar as closely as possible with the solar year. Three hundred and sixty days is much closer to the latter's duration than the 400 days that the vigesimal system would have imposed. To make the agreement more perfect, the Maya added to the eighteen months of twenty days an additional period of five days called *uayeb*, which gave a year of 365 days. This year was called *haab*.

Parallel with this solar calendar, the Maya used a sacred calendar of 260 days, called *tzolkin*. The 260 days were divided into twenty periods of thirteen days, which were called by the names of the days of the solar month in the same order. In each period the names were preceded by a number indicating their position from 1 to 13, the day *ik*, marking the beginning of the first period. We have therefore: 1 *ik*, 2 *akbal*, 3 *kan*, etc. . . . 13 *ix*. The first day of the second period was 1 *men*, the second 2 *cib*, and so on. The recurrence of the numbering 1 *ik* could not take place until the first day of the second *tzolkin*, that is to say, after 260 days.

The designation of a determined date comprised two necessary indications: on one hand its position in the religious year and on the other its position in the solar year. Therefore we have, for example, 4 *kan* 2 *pop*, which gives the position of the day in relation to the two calendars at the same time.

Morley, to make this system comprehensible, imagines two cogwheels, one having 260 cogs, the other 365, the first corresponding to the *tzolkin* year, the second to the *haab* year, each of the cogs in the first wheel corresponding to the days of the sacred year, in the second to the days of the solar year (p. 69). If we engage the two wheels so that the cog corresponding to 2 *ik* of the *tzolkin* wheel fits the space between the cogs corresponding to 0 *pop*, first day of the Mayan year on the *haab* wheel, and if we turn the first

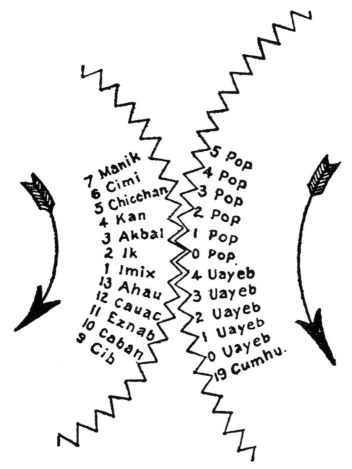

Diagram showing the correspondence of the days of the year with 365 days (haab), represented by the cog-wheel on the right, with the days of the year with 260 days (tzolkin), represented by the left-hand wheel, after Morley.

wheel in a clockwise direction and the second wheel anti-clockwise, it is found that only fifty-two days out of the 260 days of the *tzolkin* can correspond to the first day of any of the nineteen divisions of the *haab*. These fifty-two days which are the days *ik*, *manik*, *eb* and *caban*, preceded by numbers from 1 to 13 are the only ones which can correspond to the first day of the Maya year or 0 *pop*. They are called the bearers of the year.

We can calculate that seventy-three complete revolutions of the *tzolkin* wheel and fifty-two complete revolutions of the *haab* wheel are necessary before the cog of 2 *ik* is reinserted in the space between the cogs 0 *pop*. To put it another way, any day of the *tzolkin* year cannot return to the same position in relation to a day of the *haab* year before 73 *tzolkins* or 52 *haabs* or 18,980 days have passed. During this long period each day of the *tzolkin* has occupied the 365 possible positions of the *haab*.

The astronomical knowledge of the Maya was remarkably varied and extensive.

The Dresden Codex contains a lunar calendar comprising 405 consecutive lunations, divided into sixty groups of six lunations and nine groups of five lunations. The duration of the lunation is made up of between twenty-nine and thirty days. The group of six lunations was calculated sometimes for 177 days, sometimes for 178 days, and the group of five lunations for 148 days. The 405 lunations added up to a duration of 11,960 days or 46 *tzolkin*. The precision of the Mayan calculations is surprising. In fact, modern astronomers set the duration of 405 lunations at 11,959·888 years. The minimal difference between this calculation and the Mayan calculation involves a disparity of only one day at the end of 300 years.

The Dresden Codex also contains a calendar of Venus, covering a period of 384 years. The durations of the revolutions of the planet repeat themselves in groups of five, each group comprising 580, 587, 583, 583, 587 days, which corresponds to an average duration of revolution of 584 days. This duration differs only slightly from that calculated by modern astronomers: 583·92 days. The Maya also knew that five revolutions of Venus, or 2,920 days, equalled eight solar years.

All the peoples of antiquity (Greeks, Romans, Babylonians, Christians, Mohammedans, etc.) began their chronology with a date marking a historic event, either attested or hypothetical: the Death of Alexander, the Foundation of Rome, the Creation of the World, the Birth of Christ, etc. In the same way, the Maya traced back the beginning of their chronology (indicated on all the documents at present known, with two or three exceptions) to an event of which we do not know the nature and which is dated 4 *Ahau* 8 *Cumhu*. This date corresponds to the year 3113 B.C., which is 3,433 years earlier than the age of the oldest document we possess: the Leyden plaque, which goes back to A.D. 320. We have seen that at the beginning of this period the Maya erected a commemorative monument, a dated stele, at the end of each *katún*, that is to say, of each period of 7,200 days, and that this custom was even extended to the end of each half *katún* and even each quarter *katún*. These inscriptions, which are so valuable in establishing Mayan chronology, comprise a series of glyphs reading from left to right, from top to bottom and placed in groups of two.

Let us borrow the example of stele 24, shown on this page, from T. Gann and J. E. Thompson. It begins with a glyph giving the name of the god who dominates the month the stele was erected, in this case the planet Venus; the second glyph is the sign of the *baktún* period governed by the number 9, $9 \times 144,400 = 1,296,000$ days; the third glyph is the sign of the *katún* period, governed by number 12, $12 \times 7,200 = 86,400$ days; the fourth is the sign of the *tun* period, governed by the number 10, $10 \times 360 = 3,600$ days; the fifth is the sign of the *uinal* period governed by the number 5, $5 \times 20 = 100$ days; the sixth is the sign of the day, *kin*, governed by the number 12, 12 days. The total gives 1,386,112 days, that is to say, 3,850 years of 360 days since the beginning of the Mayan era plus 112 days. Then follows the glyph of the day *Eb*, governed by the number 4, marking the date 4 *Eb*, in the religious year of 260 days, the glyph of the god

NARANJO. Inscription from Stele 24. (After Morley.)

dominating the night of this day, a glyph of unknown significance, a glyph governed by the number 18, which means that the date of the monument fell eighteen days after the new moon, a glyph indicating that the lunation was the first in the series of six, a glyph specifying that the lunation was of twenty-nine days, finally a last glyph, corresponding to the month *Yax*, governed by the number 10 and indicating that the date was 10 *Yax* in the year of 365 days.

Gann and Thompson translate the inscription as follows:

'The morning star was the patron of the date that is given below. 3,850 years of 360 days have passed since the date 4 Ahau 8 Cumhu (when the world was re-created?) and in addition 112 days. The day in our sacred calendar of 260 days is 4 Eb, and in our year of 365 days the position on which this date falls is 10 Yax. The patron god of the night on which this day falls is —. This date is 18 days after a new moon, and this moon, which is of 29 days, is the first of our lunar cycle of six.'

Archaeologists have adopted the custom of summarizing the inscriptions in an expeditious and abridged form. The inscription we have just examined is thus transcribed:

9, 12, 10, 5, 12, 4 Eb. 10 Yax.

The parallel between this system and our own is remarkable, as Morley has pointed out. When we write: Tuesday, 11 August 1953, we intend to say that one period of 1,000 years has passed, nine periods of 100 years, five periods of ten years and three periods of one year since the Birth of Christ, a total which results in a determined day, Tuesday, which is the eleventh day of the month of August. To carry the comparison further we can add that this day corresponds to the second day of the new moon and belongs to the eighth lunation of the year.

The exactitude of Mayan chronology, as we have just depicted it, should make it relatively easy to establish a certain correlation between it and Gregorian chronology, because, thanks to the chroniclers and to the evangelists of the conquest, we possess many examples where the Mayan date has been recorded at the side of the European date. Unfortunately the facts of the matter are not so simple. The Maya did not use the precise system just described up to the very end. To shorten their inscriptions, they substituted a simpler system as from the beginning of the great period of the Old Empire in 731. In this new method, the inscription 9.16.0.0.0. 2 Ahau, 13 Tzec which required ten hieroglyphics was reduced to Natún 16, 2 Ahau, 13 Tzec.

In the last period of the New Empire an even greater simplification was adopted. It consisted of suppressing all indications except the glyph 2 Ahau. The inscription was limited to specifying that the terminal day of the katún was 2 Ahau. But this eventually could occur every $25\frac{1}{4}$ years, in 751, in 1007, in 1263, in 1520.

It is naturally this 'short system' which is found in the documents from indigenous sources, written, after the conquest, in Mayan language and in Latin characters: the books of Chilam Balam, the Popol Vuh and the Anales de los Cakchiqueles.

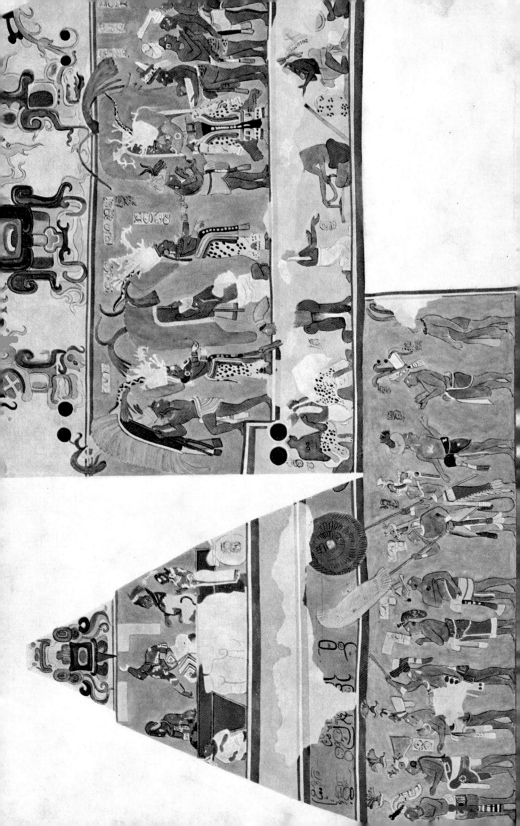

PLATE III—BONAMPAK. ROOM 1. Frescoes from the western wall and from the northern wall which is broken by the entrance door, representing, below, personages matching the string of musicians of the eastern wall; the upper part of the western wall is decorated with a stone throne on which three high-ranking women sit and the upper part of the northern wall with three personages magnificently clad. Around them servants hurry about their business and at their feet individuals, seated or kneeling, bring offerings. (Carnegie Institution of Washington, Department of Archaeology. Photo by Giles G. Healey, from reproductions by Antonio Tejeda.)

We know fragments of ten or twelve books of *Chilam Balam*
(*Chilán* or *Chilam*, soothsayer, *Balam*, jaguar, a mysterious or
occult thing, which Morley translates: 'Book of the soothsayer, of
occult things'). They are designated by the names of the places
where they were discovered; the most important are those of
Mani, Tizimin, Chumayel, Kaua, Ixil and Tusik and the *Códice
Pérez*, which contains copies of lost collections. These precious
manuscripts are at present preserved in the Library of the University of Philadelphia.

The most important part of these books is constituted by the
u kahlay katunob, indigenous chronicles where the principal events
of Mayan history are summarized *katún* by *katún*.

The *Popol Vuh* or 'Book of the Quiche' deals with the history
of the Mayan populations from the southern territories, the Kiče.
The original manuscript of this work was found in 1928, by Walter
Lehmann in the Ayer Collection of the Newberry Library of Chicago.

The *Anales de los Cakchiqueles* cover a more extensive period of
history of the *Kakčikel*. This document is preserved at the Library
of the University of Philadelphia.

All these documents have great value, but we can imagine the
difficulties they present to archaeologists who have tried to establish
a correlation between the shortened notation to which they refer
and the explicit notation of the Old Empire. Few labours have dis-
played more patience and at the same time more ingenuity on the
part of researchers. Agreement has not yet been reached between
them, but it can be said that the exact solution is already enclosed
in the figures which they have arrived at.

We know for example that one *katún*, 13 *Ahau* of the shortened
notation came to an end during the course of the year 1539. The
whole question is to know to which *katún*, 13 *Ahau* of the old
notation it corresponds exactly. J. T. Goodman believes that the
end of this *katún* fell on 14 November 1539 and that its complete
designation is 11.16.0.0.0. 13 *Ahau* 8 *Xul*. This date is 94,799 days
in advance of that proposed by H. Spinden and Hans Ludendorff,
and 42,644 days behind that put forward by Damian Kreichgauer.
It is Goodman's chronology that we have adopted here.

RELIGION

The Maya worshipped a supreme being, the creator of the world,
called *Hunab*. They believed in the existence of successive worlds,
each of which had been destroyed by a flood. The secondary gods,

who were more intimately connected with daily life, were either benevolent or malevolent. The former produced thunder, lightning and rain, favoured the harvesting of the maize and averted famines; the latter were the instigators of droughts, hurricanes and war, with their resulting misery and hardship.

The Maya conceived of the world as composed of thirteen skies, each one on top of another, and each one governed by one god.

Besides these, there were nine lower worlds, in a similar hierarchy, each with its special god, the nethermost being directed by *Ah Puch*, or the lord of death.

The Indians invoked or appeased all these gods by multiple ceremonies. These all began with periods of abstinence and continence, sometimes of very long duration. The fast consisted of the absence of meat, salt and pimento from the diet. After this form of purification came the offerings: various foodstuffs, maize tortillas, beans, honey, incense, tobacco, the firstfruits of the harvest, animals, living or dead, cooked or raw, jade or shell, beads, pendants, feathers, jaguar skin, etc.

The offerings were naturally in proportion to the importance of the favour demanded, personally or collectively.

A frequent sacrifice was to draw blood from the lobe of the ear, the nose, forehead, cheek, lower lip, arm, leg or genital organs. The idols were sprinkled with this blood.

Copal appeared at all the ceremonies; it was burnt in special censers.

Dancing was a religious rite. Each sex had its own dances. The participants were often masked.

The musical instruments used by the Maya were a wooden drum, a tortoise shell beaten with the antlers of a stag, a trumpet made of a sea-shell, flutes with five holes made from wood, rushes, bone or pottery, whistles, large wooden trumpets, cattle bells and the musical bow. It does not seem as though the art of music was very highly developed amongst the Maya.

The Indians believed in the continuation of life after death, either in a place of pleasure and abundance or of suffering situated in the ninth lower world or *Mitmal*.

The great god or *Hunab Ku* did not play an important role in the religious life of the people.

His son *Itzamná* is represented as a toothless old man with hollow cheeks, aquiline nose, and quite often with a beard. This was the god of the skies, the night and the day. *Itzamná* was intimately associated with the sun god, *Kinich Aham*, and with his wife the moon goddess *Ixchel*. He was said to have been the first priest and the inventor of writing. He was essentially the benevolent god.

Chac, the god of rain, is represented in the Codex and in architectural decoration (Figs. 5, 9, 12, 15, 16, 17, 21, 93, 114, 118) with a long nose, similar to an elephant's trunk and two prominent teeth; he wears a knotted band round his head. He was certainly a very great god, presiding over wind, the thunder and lightning as well as rain. He became, as a result, the god of fertility and agriculture. He divided himself as it were into four representations, corresponding to the four cardinal points, each having a special colour: red for east, white for north, black for west, yellow for south. *Chac* was *par excellence* the friend of man.

The god of maize is shown in the Codex as an adolescent; his head was often decorated with an ear of maize and his skull showed a very pronounced deformation. He was the patron of cultivation, the god of life and abundance.

The god of death, *Ah Puch*, was represented by a skeleton with bell ornaments as accessories. For the Maya, all evil, and in particular the supreme evil, death, issued from *Ah Puch*. He was the most malevolent of gods, associated with the god of war and human sacrifices. He was often accompanied by a dog, a *moán* bird and an owl, all three considered animals of evil omen.

Xamán Ek, the god of the Pole Star, was always depicted with a snub-nosed face and black patches on his head. He was a protecting god.

Ek Chuah, the black captain of death, was characterized by a heavy drooping lower lip and a body painted black. He must have had a dual character: as god of war he was malevolent but as god of the merchants he was benevolent. In his first role he appeared with a spear in his hand, in his second with a bundle of merchandise on his shoulders. Eminently polyvalent, he was also the patron of cocoa, and cultivators with plantations of this tree paid him especial homage.

The god of war, of human sacrifices and of violent death had a black line passing round his eye socket on the outside and continuing on his cheek. He appeared in company with *Ah Puch* at scenes of human sacrifices. Besides this, he also burnt and demolished houses.

The god of wind was closely associated with *Chac*, the god of rain. He was a benevolent god.

Ixchel, on the other hand, was hostile. She was the goddess of floods. However, in the role of wife to *Itzamná*, the lord of the sky, god of the sun, it appears she was also goddess of the moon, of pregnancy and of the art of weaving, and consequently favourable to mankind. Nevertheless, on the Codex she is generally portrayed in her destructive functions, as an old woman in a rage, surrounded by symbols of death and destruction, her head surmounted by a coiled serpent, bones embroidered on her skirt and feline claws instead of nails.

Ixtab was the goddess of suicide. On the Dresden Codex, she is represented hanging from the sky by a rope wound round her neck. The Maya had the idea that suicides went directly to heaven.

Each of the thirteen upper worlds and the nine lower worlds had its god, who bore the general name of *Oxlahuntikú* in the first case, and *Bolontikú* in the second. Of the latter, we know that each of them was the patron of one of the days of the Mayan calendar and that their succession in this role repeated itself in an indefinite fashion. Similarly, there were thirteen patrons of the thirteen different *katún* or periods of twenty years and nineteen patrons of the eighteen months and of the supplementary period of five days of the Mayan year. Thus: the sun for the month *Yaxkin*, the moon for the month *Chen*, the planet Venus for the month *Yax*, the jaguar for the month *Pop*, the bat for the month *Zotz*, the toad for the month *Zac*, the sign of the ceremony of fire for the month *Ceh*, the sign of the day *Ik* for the month *Mac*. Finally there were twenty patrons for the twenty Mayan days: *Itzamná* for the day *Ahau*, *Chac* for the day *Ik*, the god of maize for the day *Kan*, *Ah Puch* for the day *Cimi*, *Xaman Ek* for the day *Chuen*, the god of war and sacrifices for the day *Manik*, the god of the wind for the day *Muluc*, etc.

There were also patrons for the fourteen numbers (0–13), for example, the sun god for number 4, *Ah Puch* for number 10, *Chac* for number 13.

The Maya pantheon, already so populated, was further complicated during the New Empire by the introduction of a divinity bearing the name of *Kukulkán*—the conqueror of Mexican origin from Yucatán. The feast of this god was celebrated on the sixteenth day of the month of *Xul*; the most important centre of this worship was *Chichén Itzá*. *Kukulkán* corresponds to *Quetzalcoatl*, the plumed serpent of Mexico.

This enumeration might appear wearisome. It is, nevertheless, essential to show to what extent the life of the Maya was impregnated with religion and how great a complexity was involved, from the very fact of their association of ritual manifestations with every act and moment of existence. These manifestations consisted of individual and collective acts. They had to be carried out at propitious moments that the priest fixed by divination; they comprised fasting, purification, prayer and sacrifice, particularly of living things: stag, dog, bird, fish. During the Old Empire, human sacrifice was not frequent, but nevertheless existed, as is proved by two figurations on steles 11 and 14 at Piedras Negras, and particularly the frescoes at Bonampak, which I will describe at length when I deal with Mayan painting. This custom spread during the New Empire, probably because of the powerful Mexican influence during this period: four scenes on this subject have been discovered at *Chichén Itzá* and two figures on the Dresden Codex and the *Codex Tro-cortesianus* which belonged to the New Empire.

The ceremony took place as follows: the victim was presented in the nude, his body painted blue, his head decorated with a pointed headdress. The place of execution was either the precinct of the temple, or the summit of the pyramid where the latter was erected; the altar of sacrifice was a heavy stone with a convex surface.

Four assistants or *chaces*, also painted blue, took hold of the four limbs of the victim and laid him on his back on the stone so that his thorax projected. The sacrificer or *nacom*, equipped with a flint dagger, opened the lower left part of the breast, put his hand into the incision, tore out the beating heart, placed it on a plate and gave it to the priest or *chilán*. The *chilán* quickly smeared with blood the image of the god in whose honour the ceremony had been celebrated. The *chaces* threw the still warm body to the bottom of the pyramid where the priests of lower rank stripped it of all its skin, except for the hands and feet. The *chilán* dressed himself in this bloody skin and danced in company with the spectators. When the victim had been a particularly valiant soldier, the scene was accompanied by ritual cannibalism. The hands and feet were reserved for the *chilán*.

Women and children were sacrificed as often as men.

The putting to death of the sacrificial victim with blows from an arrow also appears to be a custom of Mexican origin, imported during the New Empire.

The *cenote* of *Chichén Itzá* has an oval opening 145–195 feet in diameter. The level of the water is 65 feet below the ground and is from 65 to 81 feet deep. The *cenote* was one of the most famous places of pilgrimage in the Mayan country, attracting crowds from the most distant regions. These pilgrimages mainly occurred when serious danger—epidemic, famine or prolonged drought—menaced the whole country. To appease the wrathful gods victims of both sexes as well as all manner of precious objects were thrown into this immense well.

Human sacrifice sometimes had a divinatory purpose. At daybreak the masters threw young slave women into the *cenote* without binding their limbs. In the middle of the day they cast a rope to those who had survived and who brought back the message of the gods to their tormentors, on the good luck or misfortune of the coming year. If none of the unfortunates survived the immersion, the master and his companions threw heavy stones into the well and fled away, shrieking.

The dredging of the *cenote* in 1905–8, by North American scholars on behalf of the Peabody Museum of Harvard University produced a veritable treasury of gold and copper objects: plaques decorated with chasing (Fig. 18), masks, cups, bells, pendants, bracelets, ear-rings, buttons, rings, ceremonial hatchets, beads from a necklace, and pendants in jade, wooden spear throwers, a sacrificial knife, fragments of cotton fabric, bone or shell, ornaments, pellets of copal and almost fifty skulls of both sexes, and some long bones. Mayan metallurgy being nearly non-existent, it is obvious that these offerings were not of indigenous manufacture. They bear witness to the fact that Chichén Itzá, like Santiago de Compostela in the old world, was a sacred place which attracted the faithful from very distant regions, from Colombia, Panama, Honduras, Guatemala, from the valley of Mexico and from the States of Chiapas and Oaxaca.[1]

One of the last episodes of the New Empire confirms the renown of Chichén Itzá as a sacred place. In 1536, *Ah Dzun Kiú*, chief of the *Tutul Xiú* tribe, settled at Mani, organized a large pilgrimage in an attempt to appease the gods. He first obtained the necessary authorization from the chief of Sotita, *Nachi Cocom*, whose province he would have to cross. This authorization was all the more indispensable as the great-grandfather of *Nachi Cocom*, then chief of Mayapán, had been assassinated by *Ah Kupán Xiú*, great-grandfather of *Ah Dzun Xiú*.

The forty pilgrims were royally received and feted for four days by the Cocomes. Then, during a final banquet, they were massacred ferociously.

The erection of the commemorative stele at the end of each *katún*, that is to say, of each period of 7,200 days, was an occasion

[1]Lothrop, Samuel Kirkland, *Metals from the Cenote of Sacrifice Chichén Itzá, Yucatán*. Memoirs of the Peabody Museum of Archaeology and Ethnology, Harvard University, Cambridge, vol. X, No. 2, 1952.

for great demonstrations which, in the course of time, were repeated at the end of each half-*katún* and quarter-*katún*. A special
idol corresponded to each of these periods and the ceremony consisted in substituting the new representation for the old.

An equally important ceremony took place at the time of the
Mayan new year. It began with a sort of general seclusion during
the last five days of the old year. The feasts which followed were
celebrated in the house of an important man of the community.
The idol, the patron of the new year, was transported there from
one of the entrances to the village, after incense had been burnt
before him and he had received an offering of a decapitated bird,
amidst dancing and general rejoicing. Once at the house, new
offerings were placed before him, and also before the idol, the
patron of the old year. These offerings were finally distributed
amongst the participants, the priest receiving as his share the leg
of a stag. The assistants cut the lobes of their ears and smeared with
the blood the two idols, which were finally replaced in the temple.

Each year was related to a different cardinal point and a specific
colour:

The year *Cauac* with south and yellow;
the year *Kan* with east and red;
the year *Ix* with west and black;
the year *Muluc* with north and white.

Other ceremonies were held at the beginning of the month to
appease or gain the favour of one of the gods to obtain rain or good
harvests, success in hunting or fishing, commerce, war and every
other enterprise.

Although very incomplete, this study enables us to understand
to what extent the Indian lived and died in a religious atmosphere.
Without exaggerating, it can be said that every moment as well as
every act of his existence was associated with ceremonies, the
necessity for which was impressed on his mind in an uncompromis-
ing manner. The day of the sacred year of 260 days when he was
born, as it were determined his destiny, decided which gods were
favourable to him and which were hostile. Desirous of having
children, the Mayan wife offered gifts and prayers to the gods so
that her union might be fertile. The new-born was washed at birth,
and, four or five days after, subjected to an apparatus for deforming his skull. This apparatus was composed of two boards, one
placed at the nape of the neck, the other on the forehead, which
were pressed more and more tightly together. The pressure produced a definite flattening. All the human figures depicted on the

COPÁN. Stele M. (*Photo Jesús Núñez nchilla.*)

[39] COPÁN. Stele H, eastern side. (*Photo Jesús Núñez Chinchilla.*)

[40] COPÁN. Altar O. Position of the Hieroglyphic Stairway. (*Photo Jesús Núñez Chinchilla.*)

[41] COPÁN. Altar Q. (*Photo Musée de l'Homme.*)

[42] COPÁN. Altar G, with Stele F in the background. (*Photo Joaquin Múñoz.*)

[43] PALENQUE. El Palacio. Building A. Bas Relief in stucco from the eastern side.

[44] PALENQUE. El Palacio. Building A. Panel with hieroglyphics. (*Photo Jacques Soustelle.*)

5] PALENQUE. El Palacio. uilding C. Sculptured Stairway. *hoto Henri Lehmann.*)

[46] PALENQUE. El Palacio. Building A. Exterior Gallery. (*Photo Jacques Soustelle.*)

[47] PALENQUE. Sculptured Bas Reliefs framing the stairway of Building C. (*Photo Musée de l'Homme.*)

[48] PALENQUE. Stucco Bas Relief from a pillar of Building D. (*Photo Musée de l'Homme.*)

[49] PALENQUE. El Palacio. Stucco Bas Relief decorating a panel. Building D. (*Photo Henri Lehmann.*)

[51] PALENQUE. Temple of the Inscriptions. The black line marks the secret stairway and the crypt with its sarcophagus. (*Photo Alberto Ruz Lhuillier.*)

[50] PALENQUE. Bas Relief in stucco. Building D. (*Photo Alberto Ruz Lhuillier.*)

[52] PALENQUE. Sculptured Bas Relief framing the stairway of Building C (detail). (*Photo Henri Lehmann.*)

[53] PALENQUE. Bas Relief from the Temple of the Sun. (*Photo Musée de l'Homme.*)

[54] PALENQUE. El Palacio (at the end of 1952). (*Photo Alberto Ruz Lhuillier.*)

[55] PALENQUE. Bas Relief in stucco. Building D. (*Photo Henri Lehmann.*)

[57] PALENQUE. Bas Relief from the Temple of the Foliated Cross. (*Photo Musée de l'Homme.*)
[56] PALENQUE. Bas Relief from the Temple of the Cross. (*Photo Musée de l'Homme.*)

[58] PALENQUE. Bas Relief from the Temple of the Foliated Cross. (*Photo Musée de l'Homm*

monuments reveal this (Fig. 10). The mothers also tried to make their children squint by fixing a ball of resin from their hair to hang between their eyes and make them converge their gaze. They perforated the lobes of their ears, their lips, the nasal division, to insert metal, jade, shell or wooden ornaments. It is probable that all these mutilations were not made for aesthetic purposes alone.

Nothing can give a better idea of the symbolism of an act than the importance accorded to the method of carrying a child. The infant was carried astride the left hip and supported by the left arm. For girls this mode of carrying began at the age of three months, because the Mayan hearth, the symbol of feminine occupations, was formed of three stones; for the boys at the age of four months, because the earth, the symbol of masculine work, had four cardinal points. All this involved a ceremonial which emphasized its distinctly religious character.

If a boy was concerned, nine objects were placed on a table corresponding to the activities of his state of manhood; if a little girl was concerned, the objects related to her duties as a woman. The father gave the child to the godfather, who placed it on his hip and went round the table nine times putting one of the objects into the child's hand at each turn. The godmother then carried out the same act, and returned the child to the godfather who gave it to the father. He and his wife knelt before the godfather and the ceremony ended with a distribution of food and drink.

The name of the new-born was given him on the fifth day from his birth by a priest who at the same time cast his horoscope and indicated the profession he must embrace.

At puberty, that is to say about the age of twelve, a great ceremony was celebrated, preceded by a fast of three days with sexual abstinence observed by the parents and participants. Everybody gathered in the courtyard of the godfather's house, boys and girls in two distinct ranks. The priest proceeded to purify the house; four assistants, seated at the four corners of the courtyard, held a rope which went round it and encircled the children; their parents and the priest were seated before a brazier and plates containing ground maize and copal. The children, in turn, advanced, received a little of these substances and threw them into the brazier. Brazier and rope, together with a little drink, were then entrusted to an assistant, whose job it was to carry them outside the village without turning back and without drinking. The demon was thus expelled from the body of the children. The courtyard was immediately swept and the soil covered with a mat. The priest dressed himself

M.C.—G

in a brilliant cloak and feathered mitre while the assistants placed pieces of white cloth on the heads of the children.

Everybody was seated and maintained absolute silence. The priest sprinkled the assembly with a sort of aspergillum on which snakes' tails and small bells were hung. Then the godfather of the ceremony struck the forehead of each child nine times with a bone given by the officiant, and moistened their faces and the inter-digitary spaces of their hands and feet with holy water. It con-cluded with a distribution of gifts to the actors and participants and with a meal and carouse in which the patron of the ceremony did not participate, as he had to fast for nine days.

Boys slept in a communal house up to marriage; they participated in the work of their father, while the young girls learned everything that was incumbent on their sex in family life with their mother.

A curious thing—the marriage ceremony was very simple. Marriage consisted of a dowry that the father of the fiancé must give to the father of the young girl. This dowry primarily con-sisted of clothes. On the appointed day, the parents and the guests gathered in the house of the father of the fiancée. The priest de-livered an address where he recalled the conditions of marriage and the total marriage sums pledged, fumigated the house, recited prayers and blessed the young couple. The ceremony ended with a banquet. The son-in-law lived in his parents-in-law's house, work-ing for them for six or seven years. If he failed to conform to this rule, they chased him from their door and sought another husband for their daughter.

Illness with the Maya required the intervention of the priest or the witch-doctor. Therapeutics consisted of prayers, special cere-monies, bleedings and the administration of various remedies.

Immediately after death, the corpse was enveloped in a shroud, its mouth filled with ground maize, with which a few jade beads were mixed, and buried in the hut or beside the hut. In the tomb, the relations placed a few clay, wood or stone figurines, and objects connected with the deceased's occupation. The house was generally abandoned. When a person of quality was involved, the body was burnt and the ashes enclosed in a large vase (Fig. 8) above which a temple was built. Sometimes also the body was placed in a vaulted tomb and surrounded by ornaments, vases, jade objects, etc. Finally, in certain cases, the facial part of the skull was preserved and the soft parts of the face replaced either by a sort of resin or by a mortar of lime moulded in such a way as to imitate the deceased's features.

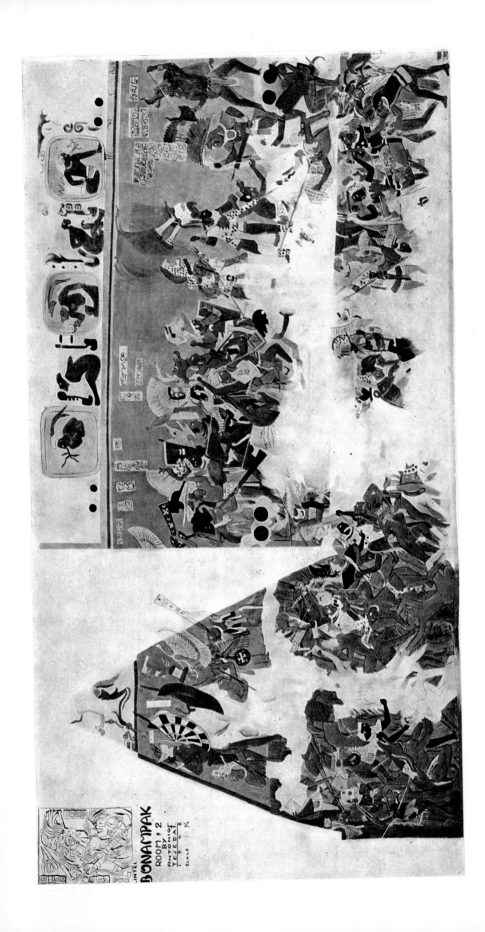

BONAMPAK
ROOM #2
BY
ANTONIO
TEJEDA
SCALE 1¼

IV

THE CITIES

ARCHITECTURE[1]

BISHOP DIEGO DE LANDA left an excellent description of the Mayan cities: 'The Indians lived in perfectly organized towns, clean, cleared of weeds and decorated with beautiful trees. In the centre of the town stood the temples with beautiful grounds; around the temples were the houses of the chief and the priests, then of the most important personages, the richest nearest to the centre, and, finally, in the suburbs, stood the houses of the ordinary people.'

We are dealing therefore with real towns in the modern sense of the word. The only difference was that the dwellings were not concentrated in blocks lining the roads and avenues, but divided into immense suburbs where each dwelling comprised a small independent farm. Also, the collection of public buildings—temple, palace, pyramids, monastery, ball court, observatories, platforms for dancing—were placed around large squares which were the religious and administrative centres of the population. It is thought that Uaxactún had a population of 50,000, and Tikal, Copán, Chichén Itzá and Uxmal 200,000.

All the Mayan buildings were built on terraces from 20 inches to 6 feet high for palaces, monasteries and dwelling houses, and sometimes reaching 180 feet in the case of the pyramids.

Temple IV at Tikal measures no less than 210 feet high, from the base of the pyramid to the summit of the building which crowns it.

The terraces were constructed of earth and pebbles and sometimes of heavy blocks of stone and mortar. The facing was made of stone masonry.

Wide and steeply sloping stairways gave access to the buildings constructed on the platforms (Figs. 11, 20, 23, 29, 81, 85, 95, 116; Pl. X). Sometimes there was only one stairway, but the largest pyramids had one on each side. Quite a wide space was left between the façade of the monuments and the top of the stairway whereas on the other sides the walls were almost level with the edge of the platform.

[1]Marquina, Ignacio, *Arquitectura prehispánica*, Mexico, 1951.

The façade of the buildings was often divided into two parts, one on top of the other, by a projecting horizontal band; a similar band ran along the upper part. These bands consisted of a row of stones in relief, covered by a layer of mortar.

The roofs were made of a hard almost flat limestone covering; the difference in level between the centre and the edges never exceeded more than 12 inches. At Copán, Uxmal, Chichén Itzá, the rain water was drained away by gutters. A wall, sometimes as high as the façade, run parallel to the façade in the middle of the roof, following the longitudinal axis of the building. This 'roof comb' was a simple ornament (Figs. 7, 11).

It is certain that these stone buildings were derived from the wooden buildings, of which the prototype was the Mayan hut, as it still exists today. The tree trunks joined at the top, in the middle and below, by three bands which formed its walls, became columns where mouldings replaced the primitive ties.

The plan of the building varied according to its purpose. A temple usually consisted of two rooms, one behind the other, the first opening on to the façade by one or three doors. It communicated with the back room, the sanctuary proper, by one or more doors.

The palaces were not noticeably different from the temples except that, in certain cases, the back room could be reached by doors in the back wall.

There were no windows, although rectangular openings for ventilation were sometimes found in the upper part of the façade.

The walls were covered with limestone stucco. They were generally vertical, although at Copán, Palenque and Tikal the upper half of the wall was at an incline.

The first buildings of the Old Empire do not seem often to have been decorated but later the upper part of the façade was covered with stucco and decorated with complicated designs and even hieroglyphic inscriptions. Except at Copán and Quiriguá, the façade was not decorated with sculpture as became common during the New Empire. Exterior decoration was effected by large mural plaques, as at Piedras Negras, or by plaques covering the ramps of the stairways. Similar sculptured plaques were rarely used for interior decorations. Mention must here be made of the beautiful specimens at Palenque. The jambs of the interior doors at Copán were decorated in this way.

With the New Empire, sculptured decoration of façades became the rule, in both lower and upper parts. While sculpture declined as an independent art form, it showed extraordinary development as a complement to the decoration of monuments. Motifs were most frequently geometric: half-columns set in the wall (Figs. 7, 9, 13, 14, 17), Greek key pattern (Fig. 9), grilles (Figs. 14, 17, 22), mascarons (Figs. 12, 15); human or animal faces sometimes decorate the upper half of the façade (Figs. 5, 17).

Large colonnades which were undoubtedly used as assembly halls appeared in the Mexican period. Some of these colonnades were from 195 to 325 feet long and comprised four or five lines of vaulted arches (Figs. 95, 103, 110, 116).

One of the characteristics of Mayan architecture is the corbelled vault (Figs. 14, 22, 46, 61). This vault was constructed as follows: when the lateral walls had reached the desired height, generally between 6 and 12 feet, each new row of stones was placed so as to overlap with the preceding row. The ensemble became a sort of stairway in reverse. As a result, the two walls gradually drew nearer. When they were only separated by a small space, a stone plaque was placed on the summit. The principal disadvantage of this method of construction was that it limited the width of the rooms. This never exceeded 18 feet.

The first example of the corbelled arch appeared at Uaxactún in 317. It is found at Copán in 435, at Oxkintok in 475, at Tulum in 564, in the valley of the Usumacinta probably in 633, at Bonampak in 692.

In 987, i.e. before the end of the Old Empire, this technique had extended to the whole Mayan territory excluding the valley of the Río de la Pasión in Guatemala.

Apart from the corbelled arch, the Maya constructed flat roofs made of beams joined by fine lath-work covered with a layer of limestone 12 inches or more thick. This method of roofing was used at Piedras Negras, Uaxactún and Tzimin Kax during the Old Empire, and at Chichén Itzá and Tulum during the New. It was undoubtedly much more widespread than archaeological evidence indicates because once these roofs have fallen in they leave no trace.

The oldest example of Mayan architecture in stone was discovered at Uaxactún. Its remarkable state of preservation was due to the fact that, after completion, probably in the second century A.D., the building was in some way topped by a masonry pyramid which protected it from the action of the atmosphere. When freed from this protective covering the original pyramid was revealed. It had four access stairways, was completely covered with stucco and was decorated with sixteen mascarons also in stucco 7 feet square. But there was no trace of painting. The upper platform had not been occupied by a stone construction, although the pyramid itself was bricked up. It showed four holes placed in a rectangle which must have held the four posts of a building of wood and straw.

The Mayan pyramids, like the Aztec, have been looked on as supports for the temples. This may indeed be true in the latter case. A sensational discovery at Palenque, which I will describe in detail later, makes it possible to state that it does not always apply in the former case, as these pyramids are sometimes funeral monuments (Fig. 51).

I do not intend to study each of the Mayan cities in detail. I will limit myself to describing four important towns, of which two belong to the Old Empire—Copán and Palenque, the third to the New Empire—Uxmál; the last—Chichén Itzá, is exceptional in that it was founded during the Old Empire, survived its fall and gained fresh splendour during the New Empire. This choice has also been determined by the fact that I have been able to visit three of these celebrated sites. Only unfavourable weather prevented my visiting the fourth—Copán.

COPÁN[1]

Copán, to J. E. Thompson the Athens and to S. G. Morley the Alexandria of the Mayan world, seems indeed to have been the scientific centre of the Old Empire. The town consists of one principal group of constructions and sixteen exterior groups subordinate to it. One of these is 7 miles from the centre of the city.

The town was probably inhabited longer than the extreme dates of its monuments indicate (460–801).

It occupies a beautiful valley 8 miles long and about $1\frac{1}{2}$ miles wide at an altitude of about 2,000 feet. It is surrounded by hills covered with vegetation, and enjoys a temperate and healthy climate.

The principal group—to which I will restrict my description (p. 107)—occupies about 75 acres. It comprises the Acropolis and five courts: the Great Court, the Central Court, the Court of the Hieroglyphic Stairway, the Eastern Court and the Western Court. It is situated on the right bank and in the vicinity of the Río

[1]Morley, Sylvanus Griswold, *The Inscriptions at Copán*. Published by the Carnegie Institution of Washington, 1920.

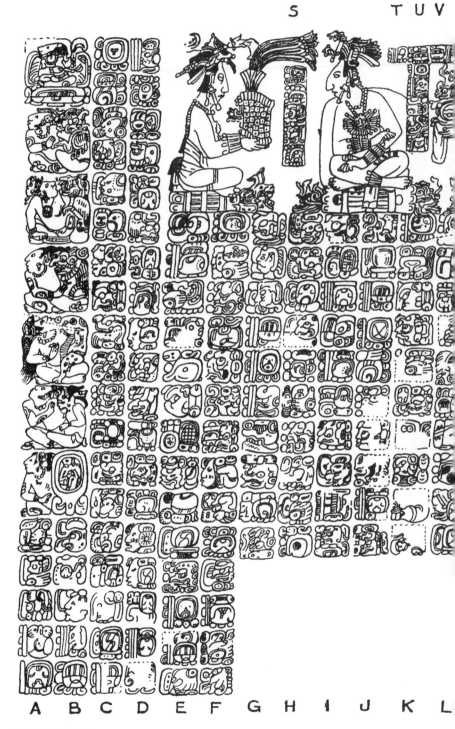

PALENQUE. Hieroglyphic panel from 'El Palacio'. Building A. (After Alberto Ruz Lh

1	
2	
3	
4	
5	
6	
7	
8	
9	
10	
11	
12	
13	
14	
15	
16	
17	
18	
19	

O   P   Q   R

Copán. The archaeologists of the Carnegie Institution of Washington in co-operation with the Government of Honduras have had to divert the course of the river to preserve the Acropolis from erosion.

The Great and Central Courts cover a vast area—650 feet, in the north–south direction, 325 feet wide in the east–west direction at the level of the Great Court, 585 feet at the level of the Central Court. This vast space is bounded by tiered platforms and by buildings 1, 2, and 3 which have not yet been explored. The pyramid with the square base, No. 4, is erected on the north–south axis. There are fourteen steles in this vast space, which I will deal with below.

The Acropolis is a large platform of more than ten acres, over 33 feet high, bounded to the north by the Court of the Hieroglyphic Stairway, to the east by the Río Copán and including the Eastern and Western Courts.

The Hieroglyphic Stairway (Fig. 30) is situated on the eastern side of the court to which it has given its name. It is 33 feet wide, including the ramps, and consists of sixty-three steps decorated with hieroglyphics, of which each one is 11 inches high and $13\frac{3}{4}$ inches wide. The ramps are 41 inches wide and are decorated with birds and motifs in the form of serpents. Six sumptuously dressed human statues are placed in the median axis of this stairway. There are no less than 2,500 glyphs; the extreme dates deciphered extend from 545 to 745.

Pyramid 26 is a tiered pyramid. The tiers of its eastern front join with those of the northern front of the Acropolis. On the side of the Court of the Hieroglyphics, its base is about 175 feet; it is 71 feet high. The temple which crowned it was reached by an undecorated stairway with eight steps, which is a continuation of the Hieroglyphic Stairway. The temple, which was small, is completely ruined. But the sculptures gathered from the debris lead one to believe that it equalled Temples 11 and 22 in magnificence. It was inaugurated in 756.

The Eastern Court measures 130 feet in the north–south direction, 97 feet from east to west. The passage leading to it from the south is bordered to the west by the considerable mass of Monticule 16, to the east by the ruins of Temple 18 (which have given the doubtful date of 767), and Terrace 17. The court itself is bordered to the north by Buildings 22 and 21, and to the south by the corner of Pyramid 16. To the east are the terraces which overlook the erosion produced by the Río Copán and where are found Temple 20 and the remains of Temple 19 which collapsed into the Río Copán before it was diverted. To the west the courtyard is bounded by the Stairway of the Jaguars and the rectangular Platform 25. The terraces surrounding the court are reached by wide stairways which occupy the whole length of the eastern, western and northern sides.

Temple 22 is constructed on a rectangular terrace 100 by 50 feet, with salients at its extremities and a central stairway. It includes a gallery surrounding a central sanctuary. The access door, placed in the middle of the façade, is 9 feet 2 inches wide and in the form of a serpent's mouth where the teeth and fangs decorate threshold, jambs and lintel. The communicating door which leads from the gallery to the sanctuary is decorated on either side with a large sculpture in relief (Figs. 25, 26, 34). This has, below, an enormous skull, on which rests a crouching personage. He himself is surmounted by fantastic animals, interlaced designs, volutes and smaller human figures. The threshold of this door is higher than the floor of the gallery-vestibule. This temple was erected in 771.

The Stairway of the Jaguars, 52 feet wide, is situated between the two slopes which border the western platform. It consists of eight steps and is decorated on either side by large sculptures of jaguars. The speckles of their fur are represented by fragments of obsidian encrusted in the stone (Fig. 24). The Stairway ends in a long landing which occupies the whole length of the western side of the court and continues in a stairway of four steps of the same width.

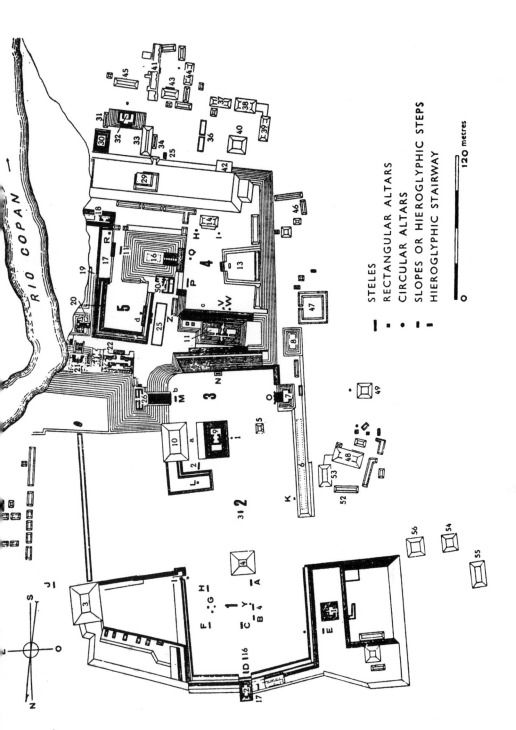

COPÁN. General plan. 1. Great Court. 2. Central Court. 3. Court of the Hieroglyphic Stairway. 4. Western Court. 5. Eastern Court. (*a*) Ball Court; (*b*) Stairway
of the Hieroglyphics; (*c*) Spectators' Gallery; (*d*) Stairway of the Jaguars. A-F,
H-J, M, N, P, 1-4, Steles; G, K, L, O, Q, R, Altars.

This stairway leads to a stylobate with a colossal head with the attributes of the planet Venus (Fig. 19) embedded in the centre. This is itself framed to the right and left by two narrow stairways leading to the summit of the terrace where Platform 25 stands, which does not seem to have borne any buildings.

The Western Court, where the ground is $32\frac{1}{2}$ feet above the level of the Court of the Hieroglyphic Stairway, is surrounded to the north by Temple 11, to the east by Pyramid 16, to the west by Temple 13 and to the south by Temple 14. It is 227 feet long by 108 feet wide.

Temple 11 or the Temple of the Inscriptions is reached by a stairway occupying the whole southern side of the Court of the Hieroglyphic Stairway. On the southern side, the building over-hangs a broad stylobate in the form of an embankment which corresponds to the northern side of the Western Court. A stairway at the western extremity of this slope gives access to it. The temple is rectangular and measures $97\frac{1}{2}$ by 49 feet. It includes two galleries facing east–west and north–south respectively, which cut each other at right-angles; both end in doors at their extremities. These four doors were decorated on both sides by a large panel of glyphs. By studying them Morley has been able to assign this building to the year 754. The two southern corners were decorated with gigantic crocodiles with their heads down and their tails up, the two northern corners with large human figures (Fig. 31). Traces of interior stairways show that the building had another floor.

A second stairway, known as the 'Spectators' Gallery', runs from the Western Court to the platform of Temple 11. Neither this nor the first stairway corresponds to the main axis of the building but to its western half. This stairway consists of five steps, the top one covered with glyphs from one end to the other; the date 771 has been deciphered here. The centre of this step is broken by a relief representing a human personage. A statue of negroid appearance is placed on top and on each side of the stairway. He holds cattle bells in his hand and has serpents wound round his body while a smaller one emerges from his mouth (Figs. 27, 28, 29).

Higher, on the platform itself, three stone sculptures represent-ing large shells are placed in the centre and at the extremities of the stairway.

Temples 13 and 14, which bound the Western Court to the west and south, are still barely explored.

Pyramid 16 is the highest point of Copán. It rises 130 feet above the level of the valley. It has a square base 143 of feet per side and consists of several storeys. The stairway to the first four is 53 feet wide; then it narrows to 33 feet up to the summit. In the broad part, the steps are decorated with skulls. The temple which crowned this pyramid is now nothing more than a heap of debris.

The Ball Court (Fig. 32), now restored, is to the north of the Court of the Hieroglyphic Stairway; it has been superposed on two previous ball courts, of almost the same dimensions, the second of which bears the date 514.

The present ball court consists of a rectangular central court, 86 feet long by 23 feet wide, bounded by a vertical slope, at the summit of which the sloping benches begin. They are 22 feet wide and end at the foot of the vertical walls of the lateral platforms. The rectangular courtyard ends in transversal courtyards at its extremities, so that the ensemble is shaped like an 'I'. Three stylized sculptures of ara heads are placed at equal distances at the higher part of the benches, near the support wall of the platform, on either side. A band decorated with glyphs in the central part of the support wall gives the date 775.

The platform which bounds the ball court to the west is wider than that which bounds it to the east. It is reached by a stairway with thirteen steps, 15 feet wide and of almost the same height. The building which crowns it consists of four rooms separated by a corridor facing west–east and of two galleries opening to east and west by three doors separated by two pillars.

The building on the eastern platform is more or less designed on the same principle, although it is smaller.

The site of Copán is famous for the number and the beauty of its steles. We know precisely thirty-eight that are designated by numbers (from 1 to 25) or by letters (A to F, H, J, and M, N, P). They are all sculptured in andesite.

All the types at present known can be found there:

(a)   Steles with one side sculptured;
(b)   Steles with the two opposite sides sculptured;
(c)   Steles with all four sides sculptured;
(d)   Steles with only three sides sculptured;
(e)   Steles with human figurations on two sides and glyphs on the other two;
(f)   Steles with one side occupied by a personage, two sides by decorative motifs and the back by glyphs.

Steles within the limits of the principal group to which I have limited my description, bear the following dates:

Stele A	731
Stele B (Figs. 35, 36)	731
Stele C	782
Stele D	756
Stele E	615
Stele F (Fig. 42)	721
Stele H (Figs. 37, 39)	782
Stele I	676
Stele J	701
Stele M (Fig. 38)	756
Stele N	760
Stele P	623
Stele 1	667
Stele 2 (Fig. 32)	647
Stele 3	653
Stele 4	782

Each stele is erected above a cruciform hollow where the faithful placed offerings.

It is not possible for me to describe them one by one. I must confine myself to pointing out that Stele B has two ara heads on its upper portion, which were originally interpreted as elephant trunks and were used to justify dangerous hypotheses on Asiatic influence in the country of the Maya; and that Stele H is the only one on the Copán site with a feminine representation.

Monuments which archaeologists term altars are very often found near the steles; there is one near Stele A where the sculptures are very faded; one of spherical form, with a round hollow on its upper part, whence issue two channels in a spiral, known as 'the stone of the sacrifices', near Stele 4; one to the west of Stele C, representing a tortoise in a basin; one rectangular-shaped with two grotesque masks, opposite Stele D; one rounded shape, dated 618, to the east of Stele E; one representing a monster with four faces, near Stele F; three designated by the letter G (Fig. 42) between Steles F and H, bearing the dates 800, 795 and 770, and representing two-headed serpents; one, rectangular, near Stele H; one in the form of a drum with a cross at its summit, to the west of Stele 1; one of small dimensions, decorated with a stylized jaguar head, opposite Stele J; one which seems to be unfinished and bears the date 762 to the north of Stele 2; one circular-shaped, dated 672, opposite Stele 1; one decorated with a serpent's head with a human face between its jaws on the northern side and with a large grotesque mask on its eastern side, near Stele M, at the foot of the

PLATE V—BONAMPAK. ROOM 2. Frescoes from the northern wall (which is broken by the entrance) representing a large stairway, at the bottom of which are shown two groups of warriors standing on either side of the door; prisoners seated or lying are shown on the steps; on the upper platform stand important chiefs surrounding the supreme chief placed in the centre and armed with a spear. This beautiful scene represents the punishment of the prisoners. (Carnegie Institution of Washington, Department of Archaeology. Photo Giles G. Healey, after reproductions by Antonio Tejeda.)

Hieroglyphic Stairway; one decorated with four figures turned towards the four cardinal points near Stele N, at the foot of the stairway leading to Temple 11.

Stele P does not seem to have had an altar. On the other hand, altars have been found which have not appeared to belong to any stele. This applies to Altar K situated to the west of the Central Court, a rectangular shaped block, bearing the date 688, which could perhaps be a commemorative stone; Altar O (Fig. 40) which is shaped like a two-headed plumed serpent, forming a seat and therefore known as 'the throne' at the foot of the stairway leading to Temple 7; Altar Q (Fig. 41), square shaped, 4 feet 2 inches along the sides, 2 feet high, each side of which is decorated with four personages seated cross-legged on cushions, in the middle of the western side of Monticule 16, which bears the date 775; to Altars H and I situated to the east and west of the northern façade of Monticule 14, all three dated 692, which are large tables placed on four stones; to the rectangular Altar Z, dated 770, to the west of Platform 25.

PALENQUE

Palenque (p. 130 and Fig. 53) is situated in the north of the State of Chiapas, amidst lush tropical vegetation. The monuments are distributed on hills covered with luxuriant forests exactly like the ruins of Angkor; their discovery and preservation have demanded the same efforts and technical ability as the freeing and protection of the Palace of Cambodia. It was at Palenque that Mayan sculptural genius reached its climax, the artists having at their disposal a calcareous stone as hard and as fine as lithographic stone. It was there that stucco was handled with the greatest mastery.

The centre of the site is occupied by a large construction, *El Palacio*. North of this rises the *Temple of the Count* which, with five other small temples, constitutes the northern group.

West of the *Palacio*, another temple still awaits archaeological exploration. To the south-west and near the *Palacio* stands the *Temple of the Inscriptions*. To the south-east a square with sides of 163 feet is surrounded to the north-east by the *Temple of the Cross*, to the south-east by the *Temple of the Foliated Cross* and to the south-west by the *Temple of the Sun*.

Other buildings, not yet explored, are buried in their shrouds of greenery.

[59] PALENQUE. Slab from the Secret Sarcophagus of the Temple of the
Inscriptions, tracing by Augustin Villagra. (*Photo Alberto Ruz Lhuillier.*)

[60] PALENQUE. Secret crypt from the Temple of the Inscriptions. Priest modelled in stucco decorating the wall of the crypt. (*Photo Alberto Ruz Lhuillier.*)

[61] PALENQUE. Crypt of the Temple of the Inscriptions with the slab again covering the sarcophagus. (*Photo Alberto Ruz Lhuillier.*)

[62] PALENQUE. Sarcophagus from the crypt with the upper part of the skeleton in place, surrounded by its ornaments. (*Photo Alberto Ruz Lhuillier.*)

[63] PALENQUE. Bas Reliefs framing the stairway of Building C. (*Photo Musée de l'Homme.*)

[64] PALENQUE. Sarcophagus from the underground crypt of the Temple of the Inscriptions, after opening. (*Photo Alberto Ruz Lhuïlier.*)

[65] PALENQUE. Reconstruction of the mask in mosaic of the skull of the secret sarcophagus from the Palace of the Inscriptions by Alberto Garcia Maldonado. (*Photo Luis Limón.*)

[66] UXMAL. Governor's Palace. Décor of the Façade. (*Photo Remondet, Musée de l'Homme.*)

[67] UXMAL. Las Monjas. Western building. *(Photo J. Kaiser, Musée de l'Homme.)*

[68] UXMAL. Las Monjas. Western building. *(Photo Henri Lehmann.)*

[69] UXMAL. Las Monjas. Eastern building. (*Photo Musée de l'Homme.*)

[70] UXMAL. Entrance door to the Quadrilateral of Las Monjas in the southern building. (*Photo Henri Lehmann.*)

[71] UXMAL. Las Monjas. Northern building. (*Photo Henri Lehmann.*)

[72] UXMAL. Las Monjas Centre Sculpture of the frieze of the western building. (*Photo Alberto Ruz Lhuillier.*)

[73] UXMAL. Las Monjas. Western building. (*Photo Henri Lehmann.*)

[75] UXMAL. Las Monjas. General view. (*Photo François Chevalier.*)

[76] UXMAL. House of the Adivino. Detail of the decoration. (*Photo Henri Lehmann.*)

The *Palacio* consists of a collection of buildings gathered on a terrace, more or less rectangular in shape and grouped around four courtyards of unequal size. These are the Eastern Courtyard, the Western Courtyard, the Central Courtyard (which is very narrow), and the Courtyard of the Tower.

The northern side is occupied by the base of a pyramid with three storeys, each 4 feet 2 inches high, the centre of which is occupied by a stairway $97\frac{1}{2}$ feet wide.

The Eastern Courtyard is bounded by four buildings.

The Eastern Building or Building A (Figs. 20, 46) comprises two large vaulted parallel rooms 7 feet 2 inches wide, divided by a wall. This is pierced in the centre by a door; its upper part, which reaches the vault, is bilobate. The walls looking out on to the exterior and the courtyard are pierced by five entrances 9 feet 9 inches wide, which undoubtedly had wooden lintels. The walls of the building are decorated with beautiful stucco bas-reliefs (Fig. 43).

A central stairway with five steps leads from the interior façade to the courtyard. The stylobate on either side of this stairway is decorated with personages in bas-relief in a style which appears archaic.

A meticulous exploration of this building, conducted by Alberto Ruz Lhuillier and Jesús Nuñez Chinchilla in 1949, led to one of the most sensational discoveries made on the site of Palenque.

The central wall of the building had fallen in a single block over a length of 97 feet. Whilst carefully raising this debris (which had clearly retained its original cohesion), the fortunate archaeologists discovered a hieroglyphic panel 8 feet wide and 7 feet 5 inches high on the lower side, in contact with the earth. It was in an extraordinary state of preservation and of execution as yet unequalled, comprising 262 signs, of which only seven are illegible (Fig. 44).

The most remarkable characteristic of this collection is that the initial series of seven glyphs, which corresponds to the year 672, is not represented by simplified signs but by complete figurations of gods and animals. Hitherto examples of this system of writing had only been known at Copán, Quiriguá and Yaxchilán.

The northern building is completely destroyed.

The western building or Building C, which separates the Eastern and Western Courtyards, is composed of two parallel rooms. They are reached by a central stairway decorated with hieroglyphics (Figs. 23, 45); the base has square panels also covered with hieroglyphics and separated by little pilasters representing personages (Figs. 47, 52, 63). The bare walls separating the entrances on the

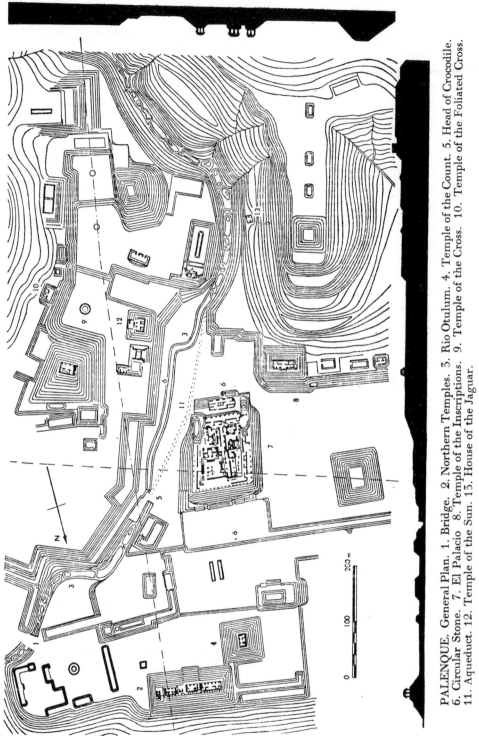

PALENQUE. General Plan. 1. Bridge. 2. Northern Temples. 3. Rio Otulum. 4. Temple of the Count. 5. Head of Crocodile. 6. Circular Stone. 7. El Palacio 8. Temple of the Inscriptions. 9. Temple of the Cross. 10. Temple of the Foliated Cross. 11. Aqueduct. 12. Temple of the Sun. 13. House of the Jaguar.

two façades are decorated with human figures in relief painted in red, black, blue and green.

The stairway which leads to the Western Courtyard is not central but placed opposite the southern end of the façade. The base of this side also has panels with hieroglyphics.

The southern building or Building B also consists of two rooms, though walls perpendicular to the façade divide them into five. Important decorations in stucco still exist there. The building is reached from the Eastern Courtyard by a central stairway.

The Western Courtyard is bounded to the west by a building designated Building D. It opens on to the courtyard by three wide entrances and on to the exterior by six doors separated by pillars decorated with magnificent stucco bas-reliefs representing large standing personages, wearing sumptuous ornaments (Figs. 50, 55).

Building E separates the small Central Courtyard from the Courtyard of the Tower. It also consists of two large parallel rooms. A door on its small northern side is reached by a small stairway from the Eastern Courtyard and is surmounted in the interior by a bas-relief of an owl with outspread wings.

Building F is on the eastern side of the small Central Courtyard. A large part of it is destroyed. The same is also true of Buildings G and H which limit the ensemble of *El Palacio* to the south.

The Tower (Fig. 54) situated to the north of the courtyard to which it gives its name is an entirely original building. It is built on a platform 23 by 24 feet 8 inches and 13 feet high. The northern, eastern and western sides of the platform are decorated with nine small seated personages, while the southern façade is occupied by an altar with three steps, surrounded to right and left by two kneeling individuals, magnificently depicted. A large stone covered with hieroglyphics found nearby bears the date 783.

No stairway giving access to the platform has been discovered.

In its present condition, the square-shaped tower measures about 49 feet, but it was once certainly higher. It consists of three storeys about 8 feet high, decorated with windows on their four sides and separated from one another by spaces of about 4 feet 10 inches where there are only skylights for ventilation. Each of these storeys was separated from its neighbour by cornices.

The centre of the tower consists of a rectangular newel surrounded by a narrow corridor. A small door in the western wall of the newel opens on to a stairway which goes direct to the second storey in a north–south direction. On the second storey a similar door gives access to a second stairway which goes up from south to north and ends at the third storey.

The Temple of the Sun (Fig. 11) is built on a pyramid with sides of 75 feet, formed of five storeys which reach a total height of 25 feet. The temple itself is 36 feet high including the roof comb which surmounts it and measures no less than 14 feet 4 inches. The access stairway is placed on the side facing east. This building forms a large square with the *Temple of the Cross* and the *Temple of the Foliated Cross*.

The temple consists of two vaulted parallel rooms, about 10 feet wide. The walls are 3 feet 3 inches thick and have three openings on the façade, the central opening being much wider than the lateral openings. The central dividing wall has a wide door giving access to the back room. This is not as long as the entrance room, as in each lateral wall to the right and left space has been set aside for a small isolated hall only communicating with the entrance hall by small doors.

Inside the rear room a wide door opens on to a small sanctuary with a special vault, placed against the foundation wall. Opposite the door the wall is decorated with a magnificent panel called the Panel of the Sun (Fig. 53) after which the building has been named. The temple is crowned with a roof crest formed by two walls thinner than the walls of the temple, between which an empty space has been left.

The wall of the façade consists of four sections separated by doors. The end sections are decorated with hieroglyphics, the two central sections with personages bearing large plumes of feathers. The sloping surface which the façade continues and which corresponds to the vault is decorated with a stucco frieze. The centre of this is occupied by a mascaron surmounted by a seated personage surrounded by masks and figurations of serpents, and the ends are decorated with two mascarons with two kneeling personages. Richly clad personages stand on either side of the door of the interior sanctuary.

The Panel of the Sun (Fig. 53) is sculptured in a calcareous stone and represents an altar surmounted by the mask of the sun placed on top of two intersecting spears and surrounded by two priests who stand on top of persons kneeling on the earth. The whole is framed by four columns of hieroglyphics.

The Temple of the Cross, which is partly destroyed, closely resembles the preceding one in plan and detail. It also houses a famous bas-relief known as 'of the Cross' (Fig. 56). The two

PLATE VI—BONAMPAK. ROOM 3. Frescoes from the northern wall, which contains the entrance door, representing below and to the left a group of musicians; in the middle, individuals sitting cross-legged and conversing together; above, important personages richly clad. (Carnegie Institution of Washington, Department of Archaeology. Photo by Giles G. Healey, after reproductions by Antonio Tejeda.)

portions of this were separated for a long time in Washington and Mexico but they are now happily reunited in the National Museum of Anthropology in Mexico.

The jambs of the entrance door of this sanctuary are decorated by two standing personages, richly adorned; the right-hand one undoubtedly represents the sorcerer-god, Itzamná, god of the night, of the starry skies and of darkness.

The Temple of the Foliated Cross is of precisely the same type. All the façade has unfortunately been destroyed but the roof comb still exists and the sanctuary houses a panel which is surprisingly similar to the panel at the *Temple of the Cross* (Figs. 57, 58). Actually, the central motif is cruciform, the symbol of the earth and life, surmounted by the sacred bird, the quetzal, and framed to the right and left by priests in hieratic attitudes, then by lateral panels containing important series of hieroglyphics.

The Temple of the Inscriptions (Pl. X) to the south-west of *El Palacio* is built on a pyramid with storeys to a total height of 52 feet. A stairway of sixty steps, divided into four groups of unequal numbers (9, 19, 19 and 13 starting from the bottom), leads to the upper platform. Here a stairway of nine steps, framed by ramps, gives access to the temple itself. The arrangement here is clearly the same as that of the temples I have just described: two large vaulted rooms, separated by a central wall. The façade holds five wide doors, which lead into the entrance room. The back room is divided into three unequal rooms, the central being the largest. On each side of the central opening are two large panels, each containing 240 hieroglyphics. Opposite this door, the wall at the back holds another panel with 140 hieroglyphics.

A wide stone slab, with a row of six perforations closed by stone plugs at each end is embedded in the soil of the vestibule. It was the starting point for a series of methodical excavations directed with exceptional skill by Alberto Ruz Lhuillier from 1949 to 1952.[1]

[1]Ruz Lhuillier, Alberto, *Palenque, fuente inogotable de tesoros arqueológicos.* México de hoy. México, vol. IV, No. 48, 1 August 1952; *Camara secreta del Templo de las Inscripciones.* Tlatoani, México, vol. I No. 3–4, May–August 1952, pp. 2–6; *Estudio de la cripta del Templo de las Inscripciones en Palenque.* Tlatoani, México, vol. I, Nos. 5–6, September–December 1952, pp. 2–28; *Investigaciones arqueológicas, en Palenque.* Cuadernos americanos, México, 11th year, 1952, pp. 149–165; *Importante découverte à Palenque dans la pyramide des Inscriptions.* Journal de la Société des Américanistes. Paris, new series, vol. XLI, 1952, pp. 583–586; *Suntuoso sepulcro en la cripta de Palenque.* México de hoy. México, vol. V, No. 55, 1 March 1953; *Exploraciones arqueológicas en Palenque,* 1949. Anales del Instituto nacional de antropologia e historia, 1949–50. México,

In effect the archaeologist undertook to discover what the slab concealed. A sounding taken very near disclosed a stairway with corbelled vaulting of which the slab obscured the entrance.

From 1949 to 1952 laborious and patient effort completely cleared the stairway, which was entirely filled with earth and stone (Fig. 51). In 1949 twenty-three steps were discovered, in 1950 twenty-three more, ending at a landing situated at a depth of 48 feet. In 1951, the explorers freed two narrow horizontal galleries 26 feet long. Two narrow openings in these gave on to an exterior courtyard, situated to the west of the pyramid, admitting a little air and light. A new stairway began at the landing in an eastward direction while the first ramp had descended westwards. This new stairway consists of twenty-two steps, the first of which goes beyond the level of the landing, undoubtedly to prevent the water which filters across the pyramid penetrating towards its base. A wall of stone and limestone closes the corridor at the foot of this second ramp. In a chest of stonework at the foot of this wall an offering was found comprising three clay plates, three shells, eleven jade stones and a pearl. Once clear of this wall, a large triangular slab was placed vertically on one side of the corridor. At the foot of this was a rough sepulchre housing six skeletons, one of a woman. This slab closed the entrance to a vaulted room, 21 feet 6 inches high by 29 feet long, reached by four steps (Fig. 61).

At its southern end, which corresponds to the entrance and therefore to the little access stairway, the width is only some 6 feet. The room itself is 9 feet 6 inches wide, but as it is enlarged in the form of a transept, it reaches 12 feet 9 inches. These lateral prolongations are not as high as the room itself. Because of the exceptional height of the vault, five stone cross-pieces set at each extremity in the wall strengthen the whole.

The ceiling of this room is 75 feet below the level of the temple and 6 feet 6 inches below the surface on which the pyramid was erected.

The walls are covered with seven stucco bas-reliefs representing a procession of nine priests, larger than life and luxuriously dressed (Fig. 60). The personages are distributed in the following

vol. IV, No. 32 de la Colección, 1952, pp. 49–66; *Exploraciones en Palenque*, 1950. Ibid. México, vol. V, No. 33 de la Coleccion, 1952, pp. 25–45; *Exploraciónes en Palenque*, 1952. Ibid. México, vol V, 1952, pp. 47–66; *The mystery of the temple of the inscriptions*. Archaeology. Cambridge, vol. VI, 1953, pp. 3–11; *La pirámide tumba de Palenque*. Cuadernos americanos. México, vol. LXXIV, 1954, pp. 141–159.

fashion: one on the northern wall, two on each side of the northern transept, one on each side of the southern transept, and one on each side of the entrance stairway. They all have large headdresses of quetzal feathers.

The centre of the room is occupied by a monolithic sarcophagus 3 feet 3 inches high, 6 feet 10 inches wide and 9 feet 9 inches long, borne by six heavy stone supports, four of which correspond to the corners and are decorated with human figures. A large slab $12\frac{1}{2}$ feet long by 7 feet 2 inches wide and 8 inches thick serves as a lid.

The walls of the sarcophagus, split in various places, are supported by buttresses which join them to the walls of the crypt. The sides of the slab are engraved with fifty-four hieroglyphics. Thirteen of these have abridged dates, which must correspond to the beginning of the seventh century, probably the year 633. The upper part of the slab is magnificently sculptured over its whole extent (Fig. 59). It depicts a man covered with jewels, his torso bent sharply forward, resting on a large mask which represents the god of the earth, death. He is staring at a cruciform motif which stands above him. This is probably a symbolic representation of life and is surmounted by a quetzal, while a two-headed serpent with small mythological beings emerging from its mouth undulates on the branches of the cross. The arms of the cross end in stylized serpent heads. A band which goes right round the slab is decorated to the east and west with nine hieroglyphics of heavenly bodies, including the sun, the moon and Venus, to the north and south with three human heads alternating with six glyphs, also of an astronomical nature.

Slate pendants and numerous fragments of jade mosaic were left on this large slab; beneath the sarcophagus itself two marvellous human heads in red-painted stucco were found (Fig. 132); under the entrance stairway were three tripod and two cylindrical vases in clay.

In November 1952, the great slab was lifted and the upper part of the sarcophagus exposed to view. A smooth stone plaque served as a lid. Its shape resembled that of a winged axe. Four perforations closed by stone plugs, as on the slab which sealed the top of the stairway, were found along the edge which, in my comparison, corresponds to the sharp edge, and one at the base of each of the two wings.

This stone which is exactly embedded in the upper side of the sarcophagus rested on a wide continuous rim, cut in the walls of the sarcophagus. The cavity has exactly the same shape as the lid. It houses a human skeleton, lying on its back, its feet pointing to

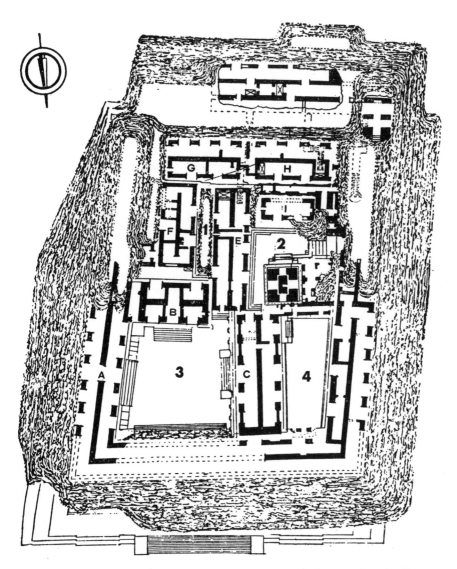

PALENQUE. Plan of El Palacio. 1. Central Courtyard. 2. Courtyard of the Tower.
3. Eastern Courtyard. 4. Western Courtyard. *A*. Eastern Building of the Eastern
Courtyard. *B*. Southern Building of the Eastern Courtyard. *C*. Western Building
of the Eastern Courtyard. *D*. Western Building of the Western Courtyard.
E. Eastern Building of the Courtyard of the Tower. *F*. Eastern Building of the
Central Courtyard. *G*, *H*. Southern Buildings. *I*. Southern Building of the
Courtyard of the Tower.

the enlarged part of the cavity (Figs. 62, 64). It was painted entirely in red. There were small disks on the skull, two cylindrical
objects through which locks of hair passed, and a plaquette with
the bat-god engraved on it. On each side were jade ear ornaments.
Fragments of a mask in jade mosaic on the left side of the head

were found. The object of this was to cover the face. It has been reconstructed by Alberto Garcia Maldonado (Fig. 65). The eyes are represented by shell plaques, with small round disks of obsidian in the centre for the irises; the pupil is represented by a painted black dot. The breast is covered with a sort of cape made of multiple beads of necklaces in all shapes. The arms were decorated with bracelets and each finger with a ring. Two jade idols were found, one at the feet, the other at the level of the pelvis.

A final detail should be pointed out because of its symbolic significance. A serpent modelled in clay emerges from the sarcophagus, mounts the length of the entrance stairway to the crypt and at the threshold turns into a sunken moulding which takes the exact shape of the steps of the stairway to end at the upper slab. Although this 'tube' does not penetrate into the sarcophagus, it can be envisaged as serving to establish permanent contact between the dead and the living. Amongst the ancient Cara of the Quito region (Ecuador) the custom existed of placing in the mouth of the corpse, once it was in the grave, a bamboo tube. The end of the tube came out of the ground and into it the widow and the relatives would pour chica from time to time. With the Colorado Indians from Ecuador, a string is tied around the body of the buried corpse and its end attached to the roof of the little shed which protects the sepulchre. It is by this means that the spirit departs. If the string breaks when pulled, the meaning is that the spirit has flown. The three customs evidently aim at the same end: to maintain a bond between the dead and those who survive him.

The fact that the sepulchre was found below the level of the soil on which the pyramid rests, the considerable weight of the sarcophagus and the slab which covers it, prove that the body had been buried before the pyramid was constructed and that its construction was determined by the especially sacred character of the priest or chief buried in the sarcophagus. The monument at Palenque must therefore have been essentially a funeral monument. It is obvious that it would be reckless to generalize this interpretation and to extend it to all the Mayan pyramids. Certain people will not fail to be tempted by this dangerous anticipation.

They will once again be compared to the Egyptian pyramids, although several thousand years separate them from the monument of Palenque. We may rely on the knowledge and prudence of the archaeologist A. Ruz Lhuillier and his team to interpret for us their wonderful discovery.

I have had the good fortune to visit the crypt of Palenque under his direction. I would like to say that I owe to him one of the greatest emotional experiences of my life as a scientist.

I will finish my description of this extraordinary archaeological site of Palenque by mentioning yet two more buildings. The first is the *House of the Jaguar* or *of the Beautiful Relief*, situated 490 feet to the south of *El Palacio*, discovered by J. F. de Waldeck. It is now almost destroyed. This temple does not measure more than 19 feet 6 inches along the side and consists of two vaulted rooms. On the back wall of the second room is a beautiful bas-relief, 7 feet 4 inches high and 6 feet 1 inch wide, representing a personage seated on a throne supported by two jaguars. From this second room a stairway with seven steps leads to a vaulted underground room.

The second building, situated 980 feet to the north-west of the *Temple of the Inscriptions*, comprises an important architectural ensemble, the exploration of which is in progress, but it has already led to the discovery of a panel, called 'The Panel of the Slaves', 9 feet high by 4 feet 10 inches wide, decorated with a magnificent bas-relief (Fig. 10). It shows a central personage receiving the offerings of two others. All are seated on top of slaves and are surmounted by eight columns of hieroglyphics. The comparison with the engraving of another plaque, also found at Palenque, is striking.

To the north of the monuments I have just described are other ruins: a ball court, situated 245 feet to the north-east of *El Palacio*, a pyramid 130 feet along the side with the *Temple of the Count* and other still unexplored buildings that are known as the 'Northern Group'.

The characteristic of Palenque is the art of stucco. It is there that it undoubtedly reaches its zenith. For a century and a half, from 642 to 783, the artists produced veritable masterpieces. The *Temples of the Cross, of the Foliated Cross* and *of the Inscriptions* that can be dated 692 are the most perfect expression of their masterly skill and their taste.

UXMAL

Uxmal was founded by the Xiú, one of the Mayan-Mexican tribes who invaded Yucatán at the end of the tenth century. The town is situated in a large valley formed by the last foothills of the Petén line of hills. The buildings are distributed in quadrilaterals without any general plan (p. 143). They are still partially covered by forest, but the most important monuments which have been cleared occupy a space not less than 1,100 yards to the north–south and 650 yards to the east–west.

They can be divided into six great groups:

1. The Palace of the Governor, the House of the Turtles, the Ball Court and the Large Pyramid;
2. The Nunnery Quadrangle and the Temple of the Adivino;
3. The Southern Group;
4. The Group of the Cemetery;
5. The North-West and Northern Group;
6. The House of the Old Woman.

The *Palace of the Governor* was probably the administrative centre of the Xiú State. It is built on a terrace with three storeys 65 feet high occupying 23,920 square yards. A stairway with three landings and edged with ramps gives access to the upper platform on which the building was constructed. This is approximately 319 feet long by 39 feet wide and 29 feet high. It is divided into three parts (the central part being by far the widest) by two vaulted corridors.

The central body is divided by a longitudinal median wall into two parallel rooms, split by partitions into ten chambers. The central chambers, which are the largest, are approximately 62 feet long. The façade of the central body is broken by seven doors, that of the wings by two doors. A wide frieze running right along the façade, above the doors, is decorated with Greek key patterns, squares and lozenges (Figs. 66, 74). The corners hold mascarons, their mouths decorated with cut teeth, very elaborate ear ornaments and trumpet-shaped noses.

The central door is surmounted by a motif (Fig. 74), representing a personage sitting on a horse-shoe shaped seat, his head decorated with a large plume. He is surrounded by eight bands in relief, ending in serpent heads. The moulding at the top of this beautiful frieze represents an undulating serpent whose head can be seen at the ends.

In Morley's view the *Palace of the Governor* is the most wonderful building of pre-Columbian times.

The *House of the Turtles* is built on the same platform as the *Palace of the Governor*, on a level with its north-west corner. It is rectangular, approximately 94 feet long, 36 feet wide and 23 feet high. It is divided in three by partition walls. The central part, which is the widest, comprises three rooms parallel to the façade.

PALENQUE. Sculptured panel of the slaves. (After Alberto Ruz Lhuillier.)

The entrance room is reached by a central door and the other two by doors similarly situated in the centres of the separating partitions. At each end are two rooms whose axes are perpendicular to the preceding rooms and these are reached by a door in the small sides of the building and not in the façade. The frieze is decorated with a line of colonnettes. The cornice which runs at the top of it is decorated with sculptures of turtles, after which the monument has been named.

North of this building is the *Ball Court*, with an arena approximately 111 feet long by 33 feet wide, then the *Nunnery Quadrangle* (Fig. 75), a vast block built on a platform reached by a wide southern stairway. It consists of four buildings surrounding a central courtyard 260 feet long by 212 feet wide corresponding to the southern, northern, eastern and western sides.

The southern building forms the principal façade; it has a wide vaulted entrance in the centre which leads to the central courtyard reached by a single step running from end to end. It comprises two large rooms separated by a continuous median wall and each divided into eight chambers by transversal partitions. Each of the chambers of the façade room opens by a door, those of the back room by openings on to the courtyard. Two small symmetrical constructions seem to have been built later at each end of this large building, forming a block 260 feet long by 29 feet wide. The frieze which crowns the walls above the doors is decorated with trellis work surrounding representations of little huts (one above each door) and surmounted by mascarons (Figs. 70, 77).

The northern building (Fig. 71) is built on a platform 325 feet long, 65 feet wide and about 23 feet high, reached from the central courtyard by a stairway 88 feet wide, framed by two small minor buildings. The building at the summit is approximately 263 feet long. It is divided lengthwise into two large parallel rooms, each of which is divided into eleven chambers opening by as many doors on to the courtyard. At each end is a double room which opens by a lateral door. The principal façade, above the doors, is decorated with a wide moulding forming a frieze of Greek key patterns, lozenges, colonnettes, human figures and birds. Each door is surmounted by a beautiful little hut or by a motif of four mascarons and by an enormous representation of the rain god (Fig. 80).

The eastern building rests on a platform approximately 7 feet 7 inches high. It is reached by a stairway from the *Central Courtyard*, 152 feet 9 inches wide. The building is 156 feet long by 34 feet wide and 27 feet high. Its two large longitudinal rooms are divided into ten chambers, split up into two bays of five, the central chamber being much the largest. The façade which overlooks the

---

UXMAL. General Plan. 1. Northern Group. 2. North-western Group. 3. Road from Merida. 4. Road from Campeche. 5. Terrace. 6. Group of Columns. 7. Nunnery Quadrangle. 8. House of the Adivino. 9. Cemetery Group. 10. Ball Court. 11. House of Administration. 12. House of the Tortoises. 13. Governor's Palace. 14. Western Group. 15. Pigeon-House. 16. Southern Temple. 17. Southern Group. 18. Great Pyramid. 19. House of the Old Woman.

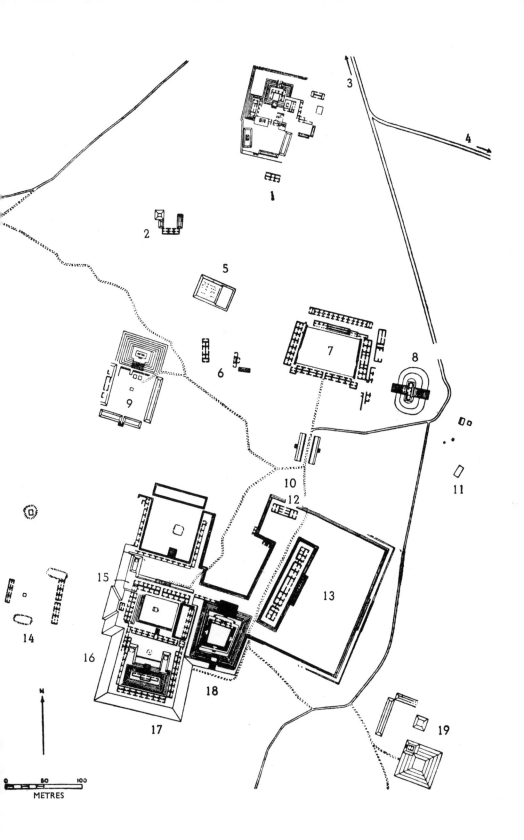

3

4

1

2

5

7

8

6

9

10

11

12

13

14

15

16

17

18

19

N

0   50   100
METRES

courtyard is pierced by five openings, the central opening being the widest. Mascarons decorate the corners and surmount the central door. The frieze between these mascarons is decorated with a trellis of squares in relief. Six groups of eight horizontal, superposed bars lie on top of this, their length decreasing from top to bottom so that they form a triangular design (Fig. 69).

The western building is 175 feet 6 inches long by 34 feet wide and 27 feet high. Its interior arrangement is similar to the preceding one. It consists of seven chambers, divided into two longitudinal bays. They are reached from the courtyard by a stairway with eight steps running from end to end. There are seven doorways in the façade (Fig. 68), which rests on a small continuous base decorated with colonnettes. The decoration of the frieze crowning it is complex. A throne with a canopy stands above the central door where a personage (now partly destroyed) was seated (Fig. 72); there is a similar but smaller throne above the two doors which frame it (Fig. 73); three mascarons above the two following doors and at the level of the northern and southern corners; a little hut above the doors at the ends (Fig. 67); finally, between these varied motifs, are panels covered with Greek key patterns and squares (Figs. 67, 68).

These vast buildings must have served as residences for the priests who officiated at the temple, incorrectly called the *House of the Adivino.* Its pyramid is situated directly to the east.

This pyramid, which is at present in course of exploration, is rectangular with rounded corners and measures about 227 feet along its north–south axis and 162 feet along its east–west axis. It consists of three storeys, the first of which is 65 feet high, the second 19 feet, the third 6 feet 6 inches. On the first landing, facing west, with its back to the second and third storeys, is a building with a double bay, reached by a large stairway 29 feet wide, bordered to the right and left by a wall separated from the body of the stairway itself, holding twelve mascarons, arranged in rows one above the other.

A rectangular temple rises on the upper platform comprising a single bay divided into three rooms. It is reached by a large stairway with neither landing nor ramp, placed on the eastern front.

The corners of the first building are decorated with seven mascarons with trumpet-shaped noses (Fig. 76). The door itself represents the mouth of a similar enormous mascaron whose teeth form the lintel. The lateral walls are also decorated with mascarons and panels decorated with square lattice work.

[77] UXMAL. Las Monjas. Southern building. Detail of the frieze. (*Photo Alberto Ruz Lhuillier.*)

[78] UXMAL. El Cementerio. Skull and Crossbones Frieze. (*Photo Henri Lehmann.*)

[79] UXMAL. Adoratorio, opposite the Governor's Palace. (*Photo Alberto Ruz Lhuillier.*)

[80] UXMAL. Las Monjas. Northern building. (*Photo Henri Lehmann.*)

[81] CHICHÉN ITZÁ. El Castillo (western face). In the background, the Temple of the Warriors. (*Photo Henri Lehmann.*)

[82] CHICHÉN ITZÁ. El Castillo. Serpent heads at the foot of the large stairway of the Northern Front. In the background the colonnade of the Temple of the Warriors. (*Photo Henri Lehmann.*)

[85] CHICHÉN ITZÁ. Las Monjas. General view. (*Photo Henri Lehmann.*)

[84] CHICHÉN ITZÁ. Las Monjas. Annexe (to the left) and La Iglesia (to the right). (*Photo Alberto Ruz Lhuillier.*)

[85] CHICHÉN ITZÁ. Stairway of El Castillo Kukulkán. (*Photo Henri Lehmann.*)

[86] CHICHÉN ITZÁ. Las Monjas. Annexe. (*Photo Henri Lehmann.*)

[87] CHICHÉN ITZA. Las Monjas. Western building. Ornamental detail. (*Photo Henri Lehmann.*)

[88] CHICHÉN ITZÁ. Frieze in relief from the Temple of the Warriors. (*Photo Henri Lehmann.*)

[89] CHICHÉN ITZÁ. El Castillo. Serpent's head, at the foot of the flight of the northern stairway. In the background, the Temple of the Warriors. (*Photo Pierre Verger, Musée de l'Homme.*)

[90] CHICHÉN ITZÁ. Temple of the Jaguars. Bas Relief. (*Photo Henri Lehmann.*)

[91] CHICHÉN ITZÁ. Temple of the Warriors. Altar with Atlantids. (*Photo Henri Lehmann.*)

[92] CHINKULTIC, CHIAPAS. Engraved plate representing a ball player. (*After I. Marquina, 'Arquitectura prehispánica', p. 660.*)

[93] Las Monjas. La Iglesia. Western front. (*Photo Henri Lehmann.*)

[94] CHICHÉN ITZÁ. Temple of the Jaguars. (*Photo Henri Lehmann.*)

[94]

[95] CHICHÉN ITZÁ. General view of the Temple of the Warriors and the Western and Northern Colonnades. (*Photo Alberto Ruz Lhuillier.*)

[96] CHICHÉN ITZÁ. Bas Relief in the interior of the Temple, on the eastern side of the Temple of the Jaguars (*After I. Marquina, 'Arquitectura prehispánica', p. 863.*)

[97] CHICHÉN ITZÁ. The Great Ball Court. (*Photo Henri Lehmann.*)

The upper temple rests on a small base with colonnettes. On each side of the door are panels decorated with square lattice work. The frieze appears to have been decorated with standing personages, on pedestals, traces of which still remain. The *Pyramid of the Adivino* is the highest construction in Uxmal and the temple which crowned it must have been the principal temple of the town. This construction covered an early temple turned eastwards.

The *Group of the Pigeon-House* is still unexplored. It lies directly to the west of the *Palace of the Governor*. It is composed of four buildings, built on a platform, reached by a stairway placed to the north and which surrounds a rectangular courtyard measuring 195 by 130 feet. The northern building, of which there only remains the central wall and the semi-vaults, which take their point of support there, has a wide vaulted entrance in the centre. The wall is surmounted by a large roof comb, its lower part comprising a series of rectangular openings and ending in triangular indentations. These have rows of rectangular alveoles and projecting stones, an arrangement which has suggested the name given to the building—the *Pigeon-House*.

The other buildings are in ruins.

To the east of this block, between the latter and the *Palace of the Governor*, rises a pyramid called the *Great Pyramid*, which has only been superficially studied by Morley; its base measures no less than 260 feet along the side.

To the south-west, west and north-east of the *Group of the Pigeon-House* are rectangular ruins which still await exploration.

The collection of ruins known as the *Cemetery* is distributed around a quadrilateral, bounded to the north by a large pyramid which measures 325 by 227 feet. A superficial exploration there has brought to light stones decorated with inscriptions in hieroglyphics, skulls and long bones (Fig. 78), suggesting the name that archaeologists have given to this building.

At the south-eastern end of the archaeological site rises the *Pyramid of the Old Woman*, with a rectangular base. Here, on a lateral terrace, are the remains of a building bearing a large roof comb. It seems that these are the oldest remains of Uxmal.

To end this description mention must be made of a whole series of ruins distributed to the north of the town known as the *North-Western and Northern Group*.

Morley emphasizes that Uxmal is the true centre of the Mayan architectural renaissance, which he calls the Neo-Classic or Puuc style, and that Mexican influence, so apparent at Chichén Itzá,

M.C.–L

is not, so to speak, present here at all. He notes the absence of serpent columns, so common in that town, the fact that there is only one small ball court, whereas Chichén Itzá has seven, and, finally, that none of the buildings in Uxmal has a sloping base, whereas this mode of construction is the rule at Chichén Itzá.

CHICHÉN ITZÁ

Chichén Itzá, termed by Morley the Mayan Mecca, belongs to both the Old and New Empires. It was founded at the beginning of the sixth century by the Itzá, who discovered it in 455, then abandoned for Chakanputún in 692 and reoccupied by the same tribe under the leadership of the Mexican chiefs in 987. The town then enjoyed a period of incomparable splendour for three centuries (the eleventh, twelfth and thirteenth). This continued under the hegemony of Mayapán despite the expulsion of the Itzá by the Cocomes in 1194, and ended with the collapse of the empire in 1441. The Itzá took refuge in Tayasal and had the honour of forming the last bastion of Mayan resistance to the Spanish invasion. It was not until 13 March 1697 that Martin de Ursua, Governor of Yucatán, sacked and destroyed it.

Chichén Itzá is approximately 3,300 yards long by 1,100 yards wide. The total surface covered is therefore about 3,630,000 square yards. The buildings which compose it can be attributed to two distinct periods: a purely Mayan period which covers the buildings completed between the sixth and tenth centuries; a Mayan-Mexican period from the eleventh to fourteenth centuries.

The first period includes the south group of buildings: *Akab D'Zib, Las Monjas, Chichanchob*: the second period the northern group: *El Castillo*, the *Ball Court*, the *Temple of the Warriors*, the *Ossuary*, the *Tzompantli*, the *Temple of the Eagles*, the *Temple of Venus*, and at a slight distance from this group *El Caracol* and the *Temple of the Three Lintels*.

Akab D'Zib means 'obscure writing'. This building has not yet been cleared. It consists of a central construction with annexes to the west, north, and south, each holding eight chambers. In the southern annexe there is a lintel bearing hieroglyphics as yet not deciphered—a circumstance which is responsible for the name given to the whole building.

Las Monjas (Fig. 83) is built on a rectangular base 35 yards 2 feet by 13 feet. It has vertical walls 10 yards 2 feet high ending in a frieze. It contains two long parallel corridors separated by a thick axial wall and ending in two chambers at either end. The large sides were pierced by five doors, the smaller by one door.

The principal façade is ornamented with large panels between the doors, decorated with four Greek key patterns framing colonnettes and diamond-shaped ornaments.

The monument is an example of a system of superposition often employed by the Maya and the Aztec. What actually happened was that the original base was covered by a larger base 54 by 29 yards, and the stairway giving access to the platform entirely reconstructed. A second storey was then contrived with access assured by a second, narrower stairway. A new rectangular building, much smaller than the preceding one was constructed on this second storey. It was composed of a single chamber with a door opening on to the centre of the access stairway.

To the east of this block and backing on to it, is a small square-shaped building containing a series of chambers. The northern façade is pierced by three doors which are surmounted by a cornice overlaid with ornaments and a frieze decorated with masks. The spaces between the doors are decorated with diamond-shaped reliefs.

This decoration continues on the eastern façade which is only pierced by one door. It is even more carefully done. It consists of two masks on either side of the opening; above this, in a circular frame, is a seated personage with a great plume of feathers on his head; the rest of the frieze is taken up by large masks (Figs. 83, 86).

A second building attached to the principal platform is known as *La Iglesia* (Fig. 84). Rectangular in shape, it opens to the west by a low door. It is characterized by the absence of decoration in its lower portions and by an extraordinary development of the cornices (Fig. 93). Large masks project their trumpet-shaped noses at the corners above a band of Greek key patterns. They undoubtedly represent the god Chac or the rain god. The frieze represents the four *bacab*—divinities who, in Mayan mythology, had the task of supporting the heavens—in the form of a shell-fish, a tortoise, a crab and an armadillo.

Chichanchob or the *Casa colorada* (Fig. 113) is composed of a base 24 yards 2 feet by 16 yards 9 inches, and 5 yards 1 foot high, supporting a rectangular building reached by a stairway without ramp. The temple is divided into two parts, separated by a wall pierced by three doors, corresponding to the three doors of the façade. The rear portion comprises three chambers. The decoration is very simple, but the outstanding feature of *Chichanchob* is that it has two roof combs, one resting on the median separating wall, the other on the wall of the façade—the latter is decorated with masks and Greek key patterns.

All these buildings precede the era of Toltec influence at Chichén Itzá.

Those belonging to the Mexican period are much more numerous and important. Some of them are examples of superposition, which indicate that the body of the town was completed over a lengthy period.

The *Castillo* or *Temple of Kukulkán* (Figs. 81, 116) is on the line which joins the two *cenotes* of Xtolóc and of the Sacrifices. This monument has been carefully reconstructed by Mexican archaeologists. It is a pyramid with a square base, 180 feet along the side, 78 feet high, composed of nine successive tiers. The temple which surmounts it is 19 feet 6 inches high. Four large stairways of ninety-one steps, one stairway on each side, give access to it (Fig. 85). The one ending at the principal façade of the temple, situated on the northern side, is the most important. The walls of the nine slopes which limit each of the tiers are ornamented in a very restrained style. This consists of projecting rectangles surmounted by a continuous moulding. Wide ramps border each stairway, ending in a large serpent head at the foot (Figs. 82, 89). The masonry surface of the pyramid must originally have been painted.

The temple proper measures 19 feet 6 inches by 14 feet 7 inches and has a door in the middle of each side. That on the northern side is framed by a portico with three openings, separated by columns representing the plumed serpent. The head of the animal is at the foot, its body constitutes the shaft and its tail the capital. A gallery 6 feet 6 inches wide goes round a central enclosure with two pillars placed at its large axis. The decoration of the façade is in very sober taste.

This construction tops an older building unearthed by skilful excavations. This also is a square pyramid 107 feet along the side, 55 feet 4 inches high. It is composed of nine tiers without decoration. The rectangular-shaped temple on the summit is divided lengthwise into two chambers measuring approximately 34 feet, separated by a wall pierced by an opening, which faces the entrance door. The entrance chamber is 7 feet 7 inches wide, the interior chamber approximately 6 feet. The access stairway has sixty-one steps and is bordered by ramps. This building is already of Toltec

NTEL

BONAMPAK

ROOM # 3
BY
ANTONIO F.
TEJEDA.
1 9 4 8
SCALE ¼

PLATE VII—BONAMPAK. ROOM 3. Incomplete frescoes from the northern wall and from the eastern wall representing, below, warriors and dancers; above, a family scene with women and servants, one of whom is carrying a child. Above and to the left, upper decoration of the entrance door. (Carnegie Institution of Washington, Department of Archaeology. Photo by Giles G. Healey, after reproductions by Antonio Tejeda.)

inspiration. A central vertical motif above the door, made of inter-
twined serpents, cuts the frieze in half. This frieze comprises four
jaguars in motion, surmounted by two large shields. The whole is
crowned by a cornice decorated with a stylized serpent and flowers.
A *Chac Mool*, a characteristic of Toltec civilization, was found facing
the entrance door, while the back room held a stone statue of a
jaguar (Fig. 98), covered by mats and large slabs. This was painted
brilliant red, with teeth cut in flint, eyes represented by jade orbs
and the spots on its fur by eighty disks of the same substance in an
apple-green colour. The Archaeological Service of Mexico had the
very happy idea of leaving this magnificent sculpture in place. It is
31 inches long, 12 inches wide, and 27 inches high. It acted as support to a disk in turquoise and shell mosaic representing the sun.
Above this was a coral necklace and a small jade head of $1\frac{1}{2}$ inches.
While the diggers were piercing the tunnel to reveal the second
building, they unearthed a cylindrical stone case containing a
precious offering. This comprised two disks in turquoise, coral and
shell mosaic, divided into eight radiating sectors, of which four are
decorated with serpent heads and four are without decoration.
The case also held two large silex knives and innumerable jade
objects.

Chichén Itzá has no less than seven *Ball Courts*. This is one of
the most obvious signs of Mexican influence. The game is actually
characteristic of Toltec civilization and has a definite religious
character. It consisted of passing a rubber ball through two stone
rings embedded in the wall of the enclosure. The ball could only
be thrown back by using the elbow, fist or hip, without using the
hands. A beautiful stone disk found at Chinkultic, Chiapas, represents a ball player (Fig. 92). The enclosures at Chichén Itzá vary
greatly in size. The largest (Fig. 97), situated in the north of the
town, is 415 feet long by 227 feet 4 inches, and the arena for the
game itself 308 by 97 feet. This court, clearly lying in a north–south
direction has the classical 'I' shape and is bounded to the east and
west by wide masonry benches, 6 feet 6 inches high, surmounted

CHICHÉN ITZÁ. General Plan. 1. Cenote of the Sacrifices. 2. Causeway.
3. Road from Merida. 4. Sacred Way. 5. Ball Court. 6. Tzompantli (Place of the
Skulls). 7. Temple of the Eagles. 8. Temple of Venus. 9. Temple of the Warriors.
10. El Castillo. 11. Administration Building. 12. Group of the Thousand
Columns. 13, 14, 15. Ball Courts. 16. North-eastern Colonnade. 17. Sudation
Room No. 2. 18. El Mercado. 19. Tomb of the Grand Priest. 20. House of the
'Metate'. 21. House of the Stag. 22. Ball Court. 23. Chichanchob. 24. Causeway.
25. Cenote of Xtoloc. 26. El Caracol. 27. Sudation Room No. 1. 28. Temple of
the Three Sculptured Panels. 29. Nuns' Building. 30. Akab D'Zib.

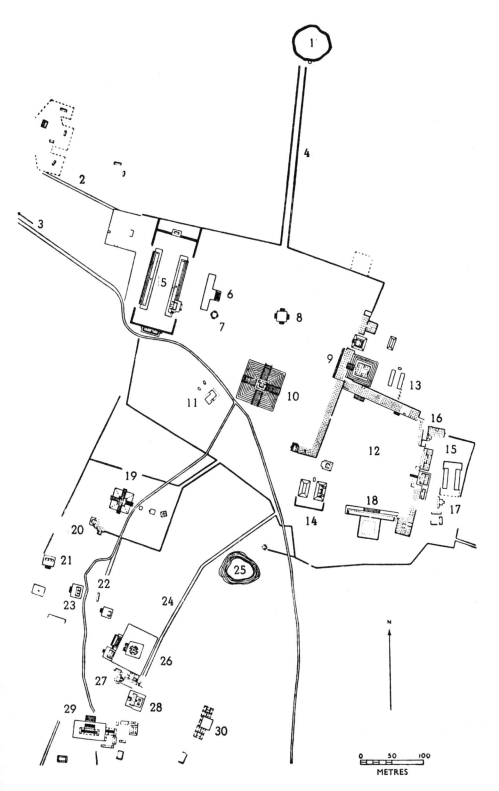

N

0   50   100
METRES

by vertical walls of about 26 feet. These run at the foot of platforms reached by immense stairways which occupy the whole external façade bounded by ramps in the form of serpents whose heads emerge above the level of the platform.

The eastern and western benches are decorated with sculptured panels at the centre and ends (Fig. 101). The central motif of these is a skull with a bifid ornament recalling a serpent's tongue issuing from its mouth. Seven ball players converge on this motif from the right and left. The first of these personages on the right is kneeling; he has no head, and six serpents issue from his neck, framing the stem of a plant laden with flowers and fruit;[1] the first personage on the left holds the sacrificial knife in one hand, the head of the victim in the other. A projecting stone ring decorated with two serpents with inter-twined rattles is embedded in the vertical walls on the east and west.

Three small square buildings stand in the centre and at the ends of the western platform. On the eastern platform there are only two. The place of the third at the southern extremity is taken by a pyramid surmounted by the *Temple of the Jaguars* (Fig. 94). This pyramid with a square base projects considerably beyond the exterior stairway as its sides measure over 55 feet. With a height of 32 feet 6 inches it also emerges well above the platform. Its summit is reached by a narrow lateral stairway and the temple by another stairway with five steps. The temple has a total height of 26 feet and comprises two parallel chambers 8 feet wide. The first of these chambers which overlooks the arena is reached by three bays separated by two columns in the form of serpents; the second chamber communicates with the first by a single central opening. The vertical wall above the portico was supported by a wooden lintel. It has a frieze decorated with jaguars, alternating with shields.

The jambs of the interior communicating door bear sculptured warriors (Figs. 90, 107). The walls of this interior chamber were painted all over. Fragments remain of a battle scene, seated personages conversing, a divinity, his head decorated with a large plume of feathers, a village with its huts and women attending to their chores. The frescoes at Bonampak also exemplify this juxtaposition of war-like and peaceful scenes.

---

[1] A beautiful Totonak bas-relief in stone represents an absolutely identical personage, giving new proof of Mexican influence in Northern Yucatán. Rubin de la Borbolla, Daniel D., *México: Monumentos historicos y arqueólogicos.* México, vol. I, 1953, Fig. 193, p. 253.

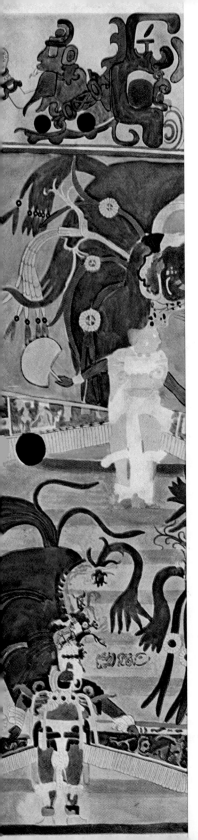

PLATE VIII—BONAMPAK, ROOM 3. Frescoes from the southern wall repre-
senting a broad stairway and dancers. (Carnegie Institution of Washington.
Department of Archaeology. Photo by Giles G. Healey, after reproductions by
Antonio Tejeda.)

Backing on to the exterior side of the pyramid is a small temple composed of a single room. This opens eastwards by a portico with three apertures separated by columns. A stone jaguar stands between the two columns. The whole interior is decorated with a magnificent bas-relief divided into four superposed horizontal bands, representing richly clad personages (Fig. 96). The ensemble was certainly painted.

At the southern end of the court, which ends in a transversal courtyard, there is another building on a platform with vertical walls reached by lateral stairways. This building is 81 feet long by 26 feet wide. Here the players could be viewed through openings arranged between six pillars with square bases. At the opposite end, on a pyramid with two storeys and a central stairway, is a smaller temple, 32 feet 6 inches by 19 feet 6 inches, composed of a single room with three openings, separated by two pillars. The ramps of the stairway represent a tree, the roots of which emerge from the god of the earth, represented by a serpent head. A branch covered with flowers winds round the trunk, where birds come to gather sap. The interior walls and the arch are decorated with very beautiful bas-reliefs.

The *Temple of the Warriors* (Fig. 95) together with the *Group of the Thousand Columns* bounds the large square of Chichén Itzá on the eastern side. This construction is one of the most recent on the site. It is a pyramid with a square base, 130 feet along the side, with four storeys. The upper platform, approximately 37 feet above the ground, bears a temple that is also square, 70 feet along the side. This comprises two rectangular rooms with vaults resting on two rows of pillars. The first room is reached through three openings framed by two pillars. A throne stands at the rear of the second room, which opens on to the first, formed of large slabs supported by three rows of small Atlantids (Fig. 91).

Each storey of the pyramid is bounded by a slightly sloping wall, supported by a broad moulding that was without a doubt brilliantly painted formerly, decorated with personages with masked profiles, armed with long, plumed javelins, as well as jaguars and birds of prey devouring human hearts (Fig. 88).

The access stairway, which has no landing, is bounded by ramps decorated with plumed serpents, whose heads emerge in high relief horizontal to the upper part. There is a *Chac Mool* (Fig. 99) on the platform in front of the entrance to the temple, and two standard-bearers on each side of the stairway. The façade of the temple (Fig. 114) comprises a slightly sloping undecorated wall below, surmounted by a vertical wall. The corners of this wall are decorated with three superposed mascarons with appendages in the shape of trumpets and frame a panel with the man-bird-serpent sculptured on it. This panel is found again on the lateral and rear façades of the building. The two pillars which frame the three entrances represent serpents whose heads serve as base, whose bodies correspond to the column itself and whose rattles form the capital (Fig. 106). The jambs of the interior doors are decorated below with a representation of the earth god, surmounted by standing personages, supporting the heavens with raised arms. The twenty interior pillars (Fig. 103) are similarly decorated but the supporters of the heavens are replaced by warriors and priests armed with spear-throwers and swords and decorated with enormous headdresses. The interior walls bear frescoes. Some of these have been restored and represent scenes from the life of a village by the sea.

Skilful excavations have shown that this temple covered an earlier pyramid surmounted by a temple called *The Temple of Chac Mool* (Figs. 105, 106). This pyramid with a square base must have measured 78 feet along the side and the temple 58 feet 6 inches along the side. It was formed, like the *Temple of the Jaguars*, of two rooms with vaults supported by a double row of four pillars. It was reached by a stairway and by a portico with a triple entrance. A *Chac Mool* discovered in the debris appears to have been placed opposite the door and is notable in that it wears a headdress decorated with a frog. In front of this buried temple, in a space 156 feet long by 48 feet wide, was a group of sixty pillars approximately 8 feet 6 inches high.

The Group of the Thousand Columns does not seem to correspond to a single building but rather to a series of successive constructions surrounding an irregular quadrilateral called the *Great Courtyard*, approximately 487 feet in length and width.

The western colonnade (Fig. 95) borders the façade of the *Temple of the Warriors* and extends southwards to a total length of 416 feet and a width of 35 feet 9 inches, the whole being bounded by a wall. It comprises four rows of columns 2 feet 2 inches in diameter and 9 feet 9 inches high, composed of square fragments, one on top of the other and surmounted by a square capital (Fig. 109).

The northern colonnade (Fig. 116) is directly to the south of the *Temple of the Warriors*. It stands on a platform 406 feet long, 65 feet wide and 7 feet 2 inches high. It comprises five rows of columns 9 feet high and 2 feet in diameter. A wall bounds the base on the northern side; it is reached by a stairway from the southern side. The columns are formed of cylindrical blocks and surmounted by a square capital.

The north-eastern colonnade consists of square cut pillars placed in five rows of ten. It rests on a platform 2 feet high, 97 feet 6 inches long and 48 feet 9 inches wide.

The eastern side of the great courtyard is occupied by various buildings not as yet explored, but where the colonnade style predominates. More to the east there is a construction which appears to have been a steam bath, and a ball court 162 by 81 feet.

The *Market Place* borders in part the large courtyard on the southern side and is more or less T-shaped. The transversal bar of this 'T' is formed by a platform 260 feet long by 48 feet 9 inches wide. It is reached from the courtyard by a wide stairway placed in the centre of the northern side. A portico runs along this, formed of a row of alternate columns and pillars 243 feet long, lined by a wall at the back and sides. The ensemble was undoubtedly covered by a continuous vault.

The rear wall is pierced by a wide central door which gives access to a square courtyard, 55 feet 3 inches along the sides, bordered by cylindrical columns 1 foot 8 inches to 2 feet in diameter and 15 feet 5 inches high, supporting a small rectangular capital (Fig. 110). These columns and the walls on the exterior frame a corridor 16 feet 3 inches wide which goes round the building.

The ensemble of the building evidently consisted of a roof supported by wooden beams resting on the capitals of the columns and the ridge of the exterior walls.

Between the large *Ball Court* and *El Castillo* are the *Tzompantli* and the *Temple of the Eagles*.

The *Tzompantli*, like the *Market Place*, is T-shaped; the horizontal bar consists of a large rectangular platform 195 feet long by 39 feet wide. The supporting wall of this platform is decorated with a continuous moulding of three rows of human skulls in relief. The vertical bar of the 'T' is represented by a short prolongation of the platform, with an access stairway, where the walls are decorated with eagles and warriors holding trophies of human heads (Fig. 104). A *Chac Mool* was buried on the summit of the *Tzompantli*.

The *Temple of the Eagles* consists of a square platform reached by four stairways placed in the middle of each side. The ramps represent plumed serpents. The four sides are decorated with wide sculptured panels depicting eagles and jaguars devouring hearts (Fig. 112).

The *Temple of Venus,* another building of the same structure, is immediately north of *El Castillo.* This name is a reference to the hieroglyphics of Venus and to the sign *Pop* which figure on the bas-reliefs of the base. A standard-bearer executed with great delicacy was found on one of the ramps of the western stairway.

The *Caracol* is one of the most notable buildings of Chichén Itzá (Fig. 100). It lies south of the archaeological zone, some 485 yards south-east of *El Castillo.* Here again we find buildings one beneath the other. The first construction was a platform with rounded corners 169 by 232 feet and 19 feet 6 inches high. Its walls consist of roughly hewn stones. It is reached by a first stairway of five steps leading to a wide landing 87 feet long by 19 feet wide. Here a second stairway of eighteen steps 45 feet 6 inches wide begins, bounded by two ramps decorated with serpents whose heads project beyond the top of the ramps.

A platform of circular design, 35 feet 9 inches in diameter and 2 feet high, was built on this first terrace. Above this stands a second platform, also circular, 52 feet in diameter by 16 feet high. At a later period a rectangular terrace 11 feet 6 inches long and 21 feet 1 inch wide was added to one side of this terrace. It finally reached its complete form of an irregular quadrilateral measuring 71 feet 6 inches on its western side, 78 feet on its eastern side and 68 feet on the northern and southern sides. The supporting wall of this work is 9 feet 9 inches high; it has a stairway with fifteen steps, 39 feet wide, erected on the west side, its ramps decorated with serpents. In the centre of this stairway a rectangular alcove 4 feet 4 inches wide was arranged to hold a stele bearing 132 glyphs.

A tower 36 feet in diameter, resting on the first circular structure, crowns this complex assembly. It is formed of two concentric walls which bound two vaulted ring-shaped chambers, leaving a circular site at the centre free for a spiral staircase. The external wall is 3 feet thick and is pierced by four doors clearly facing towards the four cardinal points. The interior wall is only 2 feet 5 inches thick and also has four doors which correspond to the distances which separate the four doors of the external wall. This is vertical and unadorned to a height of 10 feet 10 inches. At this level a projecting cornice 4 feet 10 inches high surrounds the building. It is decorated above each door by a large mascaron and a seated personage, framed by feathers and serpents. Above the frieze, the tower continues as far as a second, less important, cornice at a height of about 11 feet. The total height from the ground to the upper border of the second cornice is 9 feet 9 inches.

That portion of the building which crowned the edifice beyond the second cornice is in a very poor state. It seems that it was divided equally into two parts by a third cornice and completed by a fourth cornice. It must have been 13 feet high. The tower therefore had a total height of some 42 feet 6 inches. At the level of the third storey there were small dormer windows, undoubtedly connected with certain astronomical directions.

The central stairway is reached by a small door 1 foot 10 inches by 2 feet 6 inches which opens 3 feet 3 inches above the level of the ground of the tower. This spiral stairway is very steep and is at the same time so narrow that it scarcely permits anyone to pass.

At the north-western corner of the first terrace, a small temple 39 feet by 11 feet 4 inches was built later. It consists of only one room; it is reached by a portico with four columns, facing south-west.

To the right of the large access stairway, another temple 45 feet 6 inches by 9 feet 9 inches was built on a special rectangular platform. It consists of two chambers, the first of which opens by a portico formed of four columns.

To the south and near the *Caracol* is the *Temple of the Three Lintels* (Figs. 111, 118), 34 by 21 feet, built on a terrace 50 by 39 feet. It also consists of two rooms.

I must mention to conclude, the *Tomb of the High Priest*, situated between *El Castillo* and *El Caracol*. It is a pyramid with a square base, 124 feet along the side, 33 feet high, with an access stairway on each of its sides, and bears a temple surrounded by a gallery with a door opening on three of these stairways and a portico with two pillars looking out on to the eastern stairway. E. Thompson in 1896 discovered on the summit of this building an opening sealed by large stones and cleared a well filled with debris in which he found seven tombs one on top of the other with skeletons and numerous objects in rock crystal, jade and shell, copper bells, etc. This well led by a small stairway to a natural cavity, the bottom of which was 78 feet below the level of the summit of the pyramid. This arrangement is not dissimilar to that which A. Ruz Lhuillier found in the *Pyramid of the Inscriptions* at Palenque.

There are two *cenotes* at Chichén Itzá: one to the north called *Cenote of the Sacrifices*, which I have described already (pp. 78–79); the other to the south called *Cenote of Xtoloc* which must have provided the town's water supply and which was reached by two large masonry stairways which wound the length of its steep walls.

PLATE IX—BONAMPAK. ROOM 3. Frescoes from the western wall and from the adjoining part of the southern wall, representing a dancing scene and a group of individuals carrying a standing personage on a stretcher. (Carnegie Institution of Washington, Department of Archaeology. Photo by Giles G. Healey, after reproductions by Antonio Tejeda.)

V

THE ARTS

SCULPTURE

THE tools used by the Mayan artists were chisels and hammers made of stone (basalt or diorite) and probably also wooden mallets.

The rock used in Petén and Yucatán was a calcareous stone, relatively soft in the first days after its extraction, but hardening under the influence of the atmosphere. In certain centres (Quiriguá, Toniná, Pusilhá), the rock was a sandy stone with the same advantages as the first. At Copán andesite or serpentine (Fig. 115) were used.

Mayan sculptures, like Greek sculptures, were always painted. The colour most frequently used was dark red, obtained from iron peroxide or haematite which was abundant in the territaries of the country; blue came next in order of frequency. The colours were powdered and undoubtedly mixed with resin from copal.

The most numerous and famous Mayan sculptures are the steles which the towns erected every twenty years, then every ten years and then every five years. It seems very likely that wooden steles preceded those in stone.

We have seen the importance of these dated steles in the chronology of Mayan history. Apart from the chronological data, the steles were frequently decorated with life-size human figures in relief, which undoubtedly represented a religious or civil dignitary of the period of the erection of the stele. These are monoliths of varying size but some of them, as at Quiriguá, reach a height of 24 feet 9 inches.

The blocks of stone were first erected barely squared off and then worked on the spot, with the help of scaffolding. It is probable that the stone was transported from the quarry to the place of erection with the help of rollers and human forced labour, as in ancient Assyria or Egypt.

The oldest Mayan sculptures are the monoliths at Uaxactún (fourth century A.D.). The personages there are represented with

8] CHICHÉN ITZÁ. The Red Jaguar, encrusted with jade. Interior Temple of El Castillo.
Photo Alberto Ruz Lhuillier.)

[100] CHICHÉN ITZÁ. El Caracol. (*Photo Alberto Ruz Lhuillier.*)

[101] CHICHÉN ITZÁ. Ball Court. Bas Relief of the bench. (*Photo Henri Lehmann.*)

[102] CHICHÉN ITZÁ. Temple of the Warriors. Western façade. (*Photo Henri Lehmann.*)

[103] CHICHÉN ITZÁ. Colonnade of the Temple of the Warriors. (*Photo Remondet, Musée de l'Homme.*)

[104] CHICHÉN ITZÁ. Tzompantli. Bas Relief representing a warrior carrying a trophy head. (*Photo Pierre Verger, Musée de l'Homme.*)

[105] CHICHÉN ITZÁ. Bas Relief from the Pyramid of 'Chac Mool'. (*Photo Henri Lehmann.*)

[106] CHICHÉN ITZÁ. Temple of the Warriors. Western side, showing the two entrance columns. (*Photo Carnegie Institution, Musée de l'Homme.*)

[108] CHICHÉN ITZÁ. High Relief at the top of the ramp of the Temple of Venus. (*Photo Henri Lehmann.*)

[107] CHICHÉN ITZÁ. Bas Relief from the Temple of the Jaguars. (*Photo Musée de l'Homme.*)

[109] CHICHÉN ITZÁ. Sculptured column from the Temple of the Warriors. (*Photo Henri Lehmann.*)

[110] CHICHÉN ITZÁ. Courtyard of the market. (*Photo Alberto Ruz Lhuillier.*)

[111] CHICHÉN ITZÁ. Temple of the Three Lintels. (*Photo Alberto Ruz Lhuillier.*)

[112] CHICHÉN ITZÁ. Temple of the Eagles. (*Photo Henri Lehmann.*)

[113] CHICHÉN ITZÁ. Casa Colorada (Chichanchob). (*Photo Carnegie Institution, Musée de l'Homme.*)

[114] CHICHÉN ITZÁ. Temple of the Warriors. External wall. (*Photo Henri Lehmann.*)

[115] REGION OF COPÁN. Statue in Serpentine. Louis Clarke
Collection, Cambridge. (*Photo Musée de l'Homme.*)

[116] CHICHÉN ITZÁ. Colonnade of the Temple of the Warriors and El Castillo (eastern front). (*Photo François Chevalier.*)

[117] QUIRIGUÁ. Altar P. Western side. (*Photo Musée de l'Homme.*)

their heads and legs in profile, their trunks and arms full-face. The feet are placed one in front of the other. The same treatment is already in evidence on the Leyden plaque (A.D. 320) (Fig. 6). After 435 the posture of the personage changes slightly by a slight crossing of the two feet. It was only in 445 that, for the first time, the artist depicted an individual with a face seen from the front. This position did not, however, become general. It was the rule at Toniná and was very frequent at Copán and Quiriguá; it is also found in half the steles at Piedras Negras, whereas it is only found once at Palenque, Yaxchilán, Naachtún and Seibal. At Piedras Negras the personage is shown from the front, seated, his legs crossed; the remarkable progress in technique can be seen in four steles from 608 to 761. The individuals in profile almost always have their heads turned to the left.

With the middle period of the Old Empire (633–731), the technique gained in refinement and the archaic character of the first sculptures diminished or disappeared. But, whereas this progress resulted in the larger centres—Copán, Quiriguá (Figs. 117, 120), Palenque, Yaxchilán (Fig. 119) and Piedras Negras—in masterpieces, in the secondary centres such as Naachtún, the sculptural style is backward, described by Morley as 'provincial'.

The culminating point of Mayan sculpture was reached during the first part of the great period of the Old Empire (731–889). Personages, full-face or in profile, standing or seated, were executed in high or bas-relief with equal mastery. But from 830 the first symptoms of decadence can already be seen. On the last dated stele of the Old Empire, stele 10 at Xultún (889), the aesthetic inspiration and technical skill are clearly declining.

During the New Empire sculpture lost its independence to become a decorative architectural element. At Chichén Itzá there are no steles. At Uxmal, on the other hand, there are sixteen, but the ornamental overload marks only too clearly the decadence of the art.

At Chichén Itzá four new varieties of sculpture appeared: the *Chac Mool*, the thrones shaped like jaguars, the standard-bearers and the *Atlantids*.

The *Chac Mool* (Fig. 99) are personages stretched out on their backs, with the top of the trunk straight, their heads turned to the right or left, their lower limbs bent, their elbows resting on the ground and their arms supporting a container placed on their abdomen. The statues are either slightly larger or slightly smaller than life-size. A dozen have been found in the town; on two of them the eyes and the nails of the feet and hands are represented by encrustations of polished bone. Generally placed on either side of the doors of temples, the *Chac Mool* seem to have been used to receive the offerings of visitors.

The thrones shaped like jaguars (Fig. 98) have the dimensions of the animal. The flattened back serves as a seat and the head is turned either to the right or left. Examples of this have also been found at Uxmal.

The standard-bearers are blocks of stone in the shape of truncated cones, nearly 12 inches in height and diameter, at the base, with a hole at the top to receive the poles of the standard. Some of them, 3 feet 3 inches high, are real human statues squatting; in this case, the pole of the standard was passed through a hollow of the hands and came to rest between the feet.

The *Atlantids* (Fig. 91) are individuals whose raised arms support the altars of the sanctuaries.

PAINTING

The Maya used painting to decorate the exterior and interior walls of their monuments, their ceramics and their *Codices*.

The colours were very varied; red, yellow, blue, green, shiny black. They were either vegetable or mineral. The painters were familiar with the art of mixing and were thus able to produce many different shades.

The oldest fresco known is at Uaxactún and is earlier than 633. The extraordinary frescoes at Bonampak[1] are contemporary with Stele I, which bears the date 785 (Figs. 121, 122, 123). Traces of paintings have also been found at Palenque and Yaxchilán.

The painted documents of the New Empire are much more abundant: there are beautiful specimens at Chichén Itzá (p. 195), Tulum, Santa Rita, Corozal, Chacmultún and Santa Rosa Xtampak.

The frescoes at Bonampak, discovered in 1946 by Giles G. Healey, are the most precious documents bequeathed to us by the Mayan painters. They were executed on a layer of lime 1·2 by 2 inches thick. The colours represented are black, white, yellow, ochre, red, orange, green, blue, with varieties of shades. The building decorated (Fig. 124) is rectangular and measures 44 feet long by 13 feet 4 inches wide. It is composed of three chambers

[1] Villagra Caleti, Agustin, *Bonampak, le ciudad de los muros pintados* (Nota preliminar de Salvador Toscano). Mexico, 1949.

CHICHÉN ITZÁ. Paintings from the southern side of the Temple of 'Chac Mool'. (After I. Marquina, *Arquitectura prehispanica*, p. 881.)

each of which has its own entrance pierced in the northern wall. The walls are vertical to a height of 5 feet 9 inches, then slope to form the Mayan corbelled vault. Their total height is 16 feet 3 inches.

On the vertical wall of Chamber 1 a vast fresco unfolds (Pls. I, II, III) the central part of which is occupied, opposite the door, by three personages—unfortunately greatly damaged—which evidently represent important chiefs. To the left of this stands a group of musicians some of whom are blowing large trumpets, others waving rattles or *maraca* or beating with stags' antlers on tortoise shells or beating a large vertical drum or *huehuetl*. Other personages, covered with animal masks and carrying large parasols, are in the background. On the right of the three central chiefs there unfolds a parade of noblemen crowned with complicated head-dresses, bedecked with numerous ornaments and accompanied by two parasol-bearers.

The sloping portion of the wall, facing the door, is taken up by a series of personages dressed in large white capes, wearing large ear ornaments, jade plaques, shell necklaces, head-dresses surmounted by magnificent feathers. All these people of quality are conversing. A storeyed platform ends the scene on the right and occupies the short side of the chamber. On the lower tier, an individual presents a child whose head bears the apparatus used to deform the skull; behind him, on the upper tier, are seated three women, undoubtedly of high descent (Pls. II, III).

On the sloping portion of the wall above the door, the three personages who, on the lower part, have been partially destroyed, are reproduced, fortunately in a perfect state; their heads are surmounted by a magnificent plume of feathers, their loins girt with a jaguar skin attached to the waist by belts covered with ornaments. They are wearing magnificent ear ornaments, breast-plates and bracelets. Servants bustle around them. The scene takes place on a platform, the pedestal of which is decorated with seated or kneeling individuals, bearers of various offerings.

All these scenes are accompanied by hieroglyphic inscriptions which should give the names of the principal individuals. If their decipherment proves possible, it will undoubtedly yield important indications as to the significance of the scene represented.

The second chamber presents on three of its walls—eastern, southern and western—a magnificent battle scene; the northern wall is devoted to depicting the punishment of prisoners (Pls. IV and V).

PLATE X—PALENQUE. PYRAMID OF THE INSCRIPTIONS. (Photo François Chevalier.)

The battle scene is divided into two levels; on top are the chiefs giving orders and wrestling; below, the mass of the troops fighting. The conflict is depicted with an extraordinary feeling for movement and life. The warriors are painted black and red, their heads topped with helmets shaped like fantastic animals. Their weapons are the spear and sword made of hard wood or *macana*, against which the combatants defend themselves with rectangular shields. In the midst of the battle, an individual is playing the horn. The essential aim of the war is here clearly apparent—the taking of prisoners. Here warriors can actually be seen seizing by the hair their vanquished enemies.

That portion of the fresco devoted to the chiefs begins on the eastern wall with three parasol-bearers beside two chiefs in discussion; a third is issuing orders with a horn.

On the southern wall, the principal warriors are represented with large yellow and green plumes, fantastic helmets, spears and shields.

On the western wall, the painted scene is very damaged and shows porters feeding the fighting-men.

The northern wall is undoubtedly the masterpiece of Mayan painting. It is decorated with a violently realistic scene depicting the punishment of prisoners. This painting has as its background the stairway of a pyramid. At the foot of this, two groups of warriors mount guard. On the upper steps the prisoners are seated, dejected and bloodstained. On the upper platform, the chiefs clad in all their insignia and their luxurious adornments form two groups facing each other. They are looking at the supreme chief, standing in the centre holding in his right hand his spear decorated with a jaguar skin; his head is topped by a sort of crown surmounted by a large plume of feathers, clad in a sleeveless tunic also in jaguar skin, his feet shod in luxurious sandals. His wrists are encircled by green bracelets; a representation of a human head hangs on his breast. The first two warriors on his left have their heads decorated with the head of a jaguar and their shoulders and chest enveloped in the skin of the same animal. They are carrying upright in front of them a feathered wooden sword or *macana*. Then come what are undoubtedly assistants or servants, bearers of fans, cloaks and shells. To the right of the supreme chief six warriors, luxuriously clad, present arms to him and the first converses with him. Lying on the bottom-most step, his head resting on the edge of the platform, a captive is stretched out at the foot of the supreme chief—a magnificent representation of defeat, suffering and resignation to fate. On a step, a bodiless head rests on a bed of leaves.

The paintings of the third chamber (Pls. VI, VII, VIII, IX) depict personages clad in the same fashion as those of the two preceding chambers. The eastern, southern and western walls are occupied by a vast stairway on the steps of which ten personages are standing in costumes of unique richness wearing on their loins an ornament similar in shape to two horizontal blades of a propeller, decorated with a mosaic of brilliant feathers. Some of them carry small fans and all have immense plumes. It is probable that the scene is related to some sort of dance. A curious scene is shown in the midst of the dancers. Two individuals are binding the feet and hands of a third; and, higher still, another man seems to be carrying a container.

The upper part of the wall represents a scene of a totally different character. Three young women are seated on a throne painted green and decorated with large red circles; one is eating the contents of a container placed in front of her, while a fat and corpulent servant, who is kneeling, hands her pear-shaped objects. The second seated woman speaks to a servant who is standing behind the throne, and the third to another servant holding a child on her knee. It is a family scene, stamped with simplicity and sobriety, in strange contrast to the violence and exuberance of the adjacent paintings.

On the upper portion of the western wall, another scene represents a group of individuals, the first of whom is waving a bell; they are carrying on a stretcher a personage clad in jaguar skin, his arms painted black.

The northern wall, where the door is pierced, is decorated to the right of the latter with two warriors who are turning towards the stairway of the western wall and, to the left, with a group of musicians. Above the door a moulding shows a series of nine seated individuals who appear to be conversing and, above these, two standing personages clad in white cloaks and bedecked with shell necklaces.

This magnificent ensemble, saved by a miracle from the inclemencies of the weather and restored with astonishing fidelity owing to the photographic technique of its eminent discoverer, will undoubtedly give rise to many different comments and interpretations. A. Villagra Caleti, who has described and published it, is of the opinion that the entire building was devoted to the commemoration of a great victory. In the first chamber would be shown the preparations for war and the election of the great chiefs; in the second the battle and the triumph; in the third, the dance, either to demand success or to celebrate success. Perhaps the day will come when the hieroglyphics of the frescoes will be deciphered and it will be possible to specify in greater detail the meaning of each of the scenes represented. The essential thing is that, thanks to Giles G. Healey and to the Mexican scholars, this unanticipated testimony should now be preserved and put at the disposal of research workers from the whole world. The artistic and archaeological value of the frescoes at Bonampak is such that their importance to Mayan history is comparable to that of the Bayeux tapestry to the history of the Middle Ages.

HANDICRAFTS

Weaving

We are scarcely familiar with this Mayan art except by its depiction on the bas-reliefs of the Old Empire or on the mural paintings and the ceramics of the New Empire.

Cotton was used to make the fabric. Spindle whorls in baked clay have been found in every excavation made, from the beginnings to the end of Mayan history. The loom was never more than 2 feet 6 inches to 3 feet 3 inches wide, and was of horizontal type. *Ixchebel Yax*, daughter of *Itzamná* and of *Ixchel*, was the patron of the art. The colours used had a symbolical meaning. Black, colour of obsidian, was the colour of weapons; yellow, the colour of maize, symbolized food; red, the blood; blue, sacrifice; green, the colour of the feathers of the quetzal bird, royalty. The dyes used must have originated from the indigo plant, the roots and bark of certain trees, the juice of certain fruit and from cochineal.

Braiding

As with weaving, we must content ourselves with the baskets and mats shown on the monuments to judge the art of braiding as practised by the Maya. Examples of identical quality are shown in the bas-reliefs both of the Old Empire and of the New. The material used consisted of liana, vegetable fibres and the leaves of certain palms.

Lapidary Art

From their earliest beginnings the Maya were familiar with this art, using jade for the most part. It began with pendants, decorated with engravings that were at first not very deep. As the technique developed, however, these turned into representations in high relief of human figures and culminated in veritable sculptures, such as the statue found in 1937 at Uaxactún, which stands no less than $9\frac{1}{2}$ inches high and weighs just over $11\frac{1}{2}$ lb. The origin of the jade utilized has not so far been discovered. The geologists think that it originates either from the south of Mexico, the States of Guerrero or Oaxaca, or from the high lands of Western Guatemala. Mayan jade, like Chinese jade, is a jadeite, but its chemical composition differs from the latter. The hardness of American jade corresponds to the index $6\cdot5$–$6\cdot8$. To cut it was therefore a long and difficult task. It was done with the help of instruments made of obsidian, a substance which can score jade; this was worn away by rubbing with gravel from the same rock, with quartz or other hard rocks. The block of jade was cut up by the movement, to and fro, of a vegetable fibre which acted as a saw, thanks to this hard gravel humidified by water. The perforations were made by twisting drills made of hard wood or bone, again with the help of gravel and water.

Mosaic

Few specimens of Mayan mosaics remain. For these the artists used small pieces of pyrites or jade.

The seven magnificent disks in a turquoise mosaic discovered at Chichén Itzá are very probably, as so many of the offerings at this sacred place, objects imported from Central Mexico, where this technique was especially developed.

Engraving on Wood

The most important as well as the oldest centre of sculpture in wood is Tikal, where the twelve doors of five temples have lintels (Fig. 126) in wood of a type of medlar tree called *chico-zapote* (*Achras Sapota L.*). They measure from 7 feet 7 inches to 16 feet 8 inches in length. Eight are decorated with engravings of religious scenes; one of them, now at the British Museum, shows a *halach uinic* seated on a throne with a magnificent representation of a jaguar surmounting him. Another lintel, preserved at Basle Museum (Fig. 125), is decorated with a large serpent whose open jaws allow the arms and trunk of a god to emerge. It is surmounted by a quetzal, its wings outspread, framed to the right and left by two important hieroglyphic inscriptions. In the centre, framed by the body of the serpent itself, a *halach uinic*, his head in profile, and his body shown from the front, carries a spear in his left hand and a small shield in his right. This work goes back to the year 751.

Sculptured lintels have also been discovered in the ruins of the New Empire at Chichén Itzá and Uxmal. Two of these are decorated with a solar disk with a human figure in the centre and another personage framed in the folds of a plumed serpent. The two personages are turned towards an altar which occupies the central part of the bas-relief.

Modelling

The Maya modelled stucco and clay. Stucco was used in the exterior decoration of the buildings of the Old Empire and, on a smaller scale, during the New Empire. The most beautiful specimens come from Palenque (Figs. 2, 3, 43, 48, 49, 50, 55, 60, 132), where the modelling of glyphs, individuals and their dress reached a true perfection.

The human heads which were found during the most recent excavations in *El Palacio* (Fig. 131) and in the *Temple of the Inscriptions* (Fig. 132) are true masterpieces, not only within the framework of pre-Columbian American art but also of universal art.

The curious crest which prolongs the protrusion of the bridge of the nose as far as the middle of the forehead is not a fantasy on the part of the artist. It represents a jade ornament which was worn by those great personages, specimens of which have been found in the subterranean tomb of Palenque.

The art of modelling lasted during the New Empire, at Izamal, Nocuchich and, above all, at Acanceh where a whole wall was decorated with various animals; bats, squirrels, serpents, eagles. It is certain that these stucco decorations were originally enhanced with colours.

Modelling in clay also goes back to the Old Empire. At Uaxactún, very crude human heads have been found. The details of the face are barely indicated and the feminine trunks are similarly shapeless.

In the great period, the technique improved. Certain works were modelled by hand, others were produced with the help of moulds made of baked clay, some specimens of which have been found.

In the valley of the Río Usumacinta the Mayan artists produced their most beautiful works. With the New Empire their mastery slowly declined. They manufactured pipes and particularly censers. These objects were painted red, olive green, blue or white.

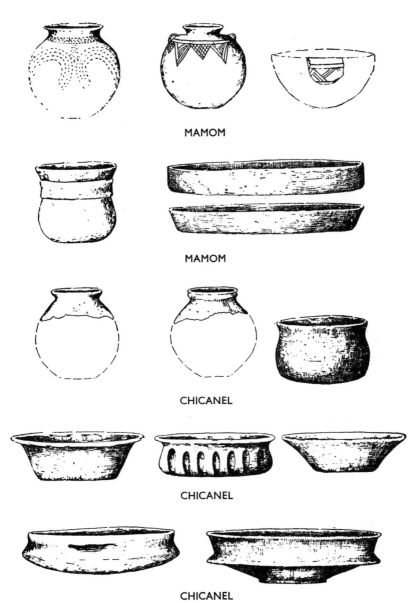

MAMOM

MAMOM

CHICANEL

CHICANEL

CHICANEL

CERAMICS OF THE MAMOM AND CHICANEL TYPES. (After Ignacio Marquina, *Arquitectura prehispanica*, p. 513.)

Ceramics

The art of ceramics seems to have penetrated to the Mayan country at the same time as the cultivation of maize, from the high lands of Western Guatemala. The oldest type of Mayan ceramic is

known as *Mamom* (p. 203). It has hitherto not been found in any
Mayan territory apart from Uaxactún (Guatemala) and San José
(Belice), but it has been encountered beyond these limits, at
Kaminal-Juyú, Utatlán and Totonicapán, in Guatemala, in the
high lands of Honduras, and Salvador and in the high plateau in
the centre of Mexico. It seems that the date of its appearance in the
Mayan country could be fixed at about the year 1000 B.C.

These grey, red, black or orange ceramics comprise large
globular pots with wide necks, sometimes with two small handles
at either side, hemispherical bowls without feet, wide round plates
with vertical or flaring edges, human heads with crudely modelled
features, with oblique, almond-shaped eyes and feminine figurines
in a very primitive style, seated or standing.

Decoration is limited to a few stripes; there is no painting. This
phase of the art must have lasted for at least six and a half centuries.

There then appeared a type known as *Chicanel* (p. 203), probably at the same time as the discovery of the calendar and Mayan
writing, i.e. about the fourth or third centuries B.C. The shapes of
the preceding period were preserved, but new forms enriched the
range of ceramics. The edges of the openings of containers are
strongly everse. Mouldings appear either along the edge or near
the base. The striped style of decoration continued but it also
comprised conical projections distributed on the bulge. Some
pottery was painted black and the process of negative painting made
its appearance.

These *Chicanel* ceramics, contrary to *Mamom* ceramics, never
appeared outside the Mayan era.

With the Old Empire ceramics of the *Tzakol* type (317–633)
appeared. They were grey, orange, red, black and their shapes
were very varied (p. 205); they were cooking pots, some with lids,
large hemispherical bowls with ring-shaped feet, cylindrical tripods, the feet of which were globular, cylindrical, flattened or
filigreed, in the shape of breasts, and bowls with four feet.

Polychrome decoration appeared and some vases have paintings
of individuals or scenes of a symbolical character.

The decorator also used incision. According to Morley, this new
ceramic was born in the Tikal-Uaxactún region, in Northern and
Central Petén and then penetrated to certain centres in the north
of Yucatán (Maní, Yaxuná, Acanceh).

The Old Empire then created a new ceramic known as *Tepeu*
(633–987). This type of pottery (Figs. 134, 136, and p. 205), is found
in Petén, and also in the north of Yucatán, at Cobá, Yaxuná, Uxmal,

TZAKOL

TEPEU

CERAMICS OF THE TZAKOL AND TEPEU TYPES. (After Ignacio Marquina, *Arquitectura prehispanica*, p. 514.)

Kabah, Labná and Sayil. They are grey, red and polychrome and come in a great variety of shapes: hemispherical vases with decorations of stripes, grooves, applied motifs, red vases with wide necks and handles, cylindrical vases (Fig. 134), barrel-shaped, tripods, circular containers with flat bottoms and sloping sides, human and animal figurines, made in a mould, sometimes used as whistles (Fig. 133), representing gods, warriors, groups of individuals in a very realistic style.

The polychrome decoration has extraordinary variety: geometric designs, human beings, animals, hieroglyphic inscriptions, ceremonies and scenes of a religious character.

From Petén, *Tepeu* ceramics penetrated southwards to the high lands of Guatemala, to the south-east, to Honduras and to Salvador. Inversely, the Petén artisans were influenced by a particularly brilliant centre of the potter's art, situated in the high valley of the Río Chixoy or de las Salinas.

By contrast, this beautiful industry penetrated only hesitantly into the north of Yucatán (Cobá, Yaxuná, Uxmal, Kabah, Labná, Sayil, Maní). The reason for this is that in the north of Yucatán, under the influence of the Mexican invasions, an autonomous, autochthonal ceramic industry had developed: during the whole of the first period of the New Empire (987–1194) it was known by the name *Puuc*. The dominant technique of this period is that of 'cutting away'. At the same time, a ceramic style spread, probably originating on the coast of Tabasco, the dye of which varied from terra cotta red to orange and which was sometimes smooth and sometimes ornamented with engraved decorations of great beauty. The dominant shapes were tripod vases with cylindrical or spherical feet. The decoration was formed of geometric motifs, but also of human and animal figures painted black.

Morley attributes to the same period the admirable human figurines in perfectly reproduced costumes which have been excavated on the island of Jaina.

The period of the New Empire, known as the Mexican period (1194–1441), is characterized by the same orange ceramics and by the appearance of a leaden ceramic with a metallic aspect. The dye here varies from brilliant orange to cinnamon or lead grey. It seems to be a ceramic imported perhaps from the west of Salvador and from the east of the State of Chiapas (Mexico). Containers in the shape of carafes with wide necks or of plates, often mounted on three legs, are frequently decorated with human or animal representations, modelled in relief.

During the same period, at Chichén Itzá as much as at Maya-pán, censers became frequent objects. These were wide containers often decorated with personages in relief, the various parts of which were executed separately and then stuck on the body of the vase itself.

After the fall of Mayapán in 1441, there was a general decadence in Mayan ceramic art which produced nothing more than ordinary works of a red colour.

Feather Work

Although not one specimen of the art of the feather has survived, it is certain that the Maya were not inferior to the Mexicans in the use they made of the feathers of the magnificent birds of their country: aras, parrots, parrakeets, cardinals, orioles, wild turkeys, ospreys, jays, humming birds, and, lastly, the quetzal, the national bird of Guatemala. The feathers were used to make plumes, toupees, cloaks and shields, to decorate spears, the sceptres of *maniqui*, baldachins, bracelets, knee ornaments, waistbelts and cotton cloths.

The characters wearing these ornaments are frequently found represented on the bas-reliefs of the Old and New Empires but the technique was certainly more skilled in the first period than in the second; the paintings at Bonampak bear witness to the magnificence of this art at the end of the eighth century.

Flint Work

The Maya attained great skill in cutting flint. They made long blades reminiscent of the Egyptian stone industry or the Solutrian industry of Europe. They also excelled in the manufacture of quite eccentric and complicated objects to decorate the ends of ceremonial staffs. Specimens of these have been found at El Palmar and Quiriguá.

Metallurgy[1]

The Maya used metals only very sparingly. They knew of copper, from which they made bells, but did not know of its alloy with tin—i.e. bronze.

In Guatemala, the Indians extracted metal from the mines of the Altos de Cuchutanes.

[1]Rivet, Paul et Arsandaux, Henri, *La métallurgie en Amérique pré-colombienne.* Travaux et Mémoires de l'Institut d'Ethnologie, vol. XXXIX, Paris, 1946.

Objects in gold of local manufacture are exceptional. They always seem to be in free gold. Most of the objects recovered from the *cenote* at Chichén Itzá came, as I have already said, from abroad: Costa Rica, Panama, Colombia, Mexico. They were offerings brought by pilgrims to the holy city. They are either in pure gold or in *tumbaga*, that is to say, an alloy of argentiferous free gold and copper (Fig. 18).

It seems, however, that some thin disks, obtained by hammering and then chased, were made on the spot, but these were works of the New Empire, and everything leads us to suppose that the Mayan artisans used an imported raw material.

The Maya used silver very rarely and did not know its alloys with copper and still less the tripartite alloy: silver, copper and gold.

A bead cut with facets at Chichén Itzá is in lead, with traces of silver, copper, gold and iron. It is the only example of the use of this metal by the Maya, although it was employed in the pre-Columbian period by the Mexicans, the Peruvians and the Indians from the Esmeraldas (Ecuador) region. Here again the object was probably imported.

[118] CHICHÉN ITZÁ. Temple of the Three Lintels. Mask of the God Chac. (*Photo Henri Lehmann.*)

[120] QUIRIGUÁ. Altar P. Northern side. (*Photo Maudsley, Musée de l'Homme.*)

19] YAXCHILÁN. (*Photo Giles G. Healey.*)

[121] BONAMPAK. Stele No. 1. On the right, Lakandón Indian. (*Photo Giles G. Healey.*)

[122] BONAMPAK. Stele No. 1. (*Photo Giles G. Healey.*)

[124] BONAMPAK. Palace of the Frescoes. Entrances to rooms 1, 2 and 3, from left to right. (*Photo Giles G. Healey.*)

[125] BONAMPAK. Stele No. 1. Central and upper portion. (*Photo Giles G. Healey.*)

[125] TIKAL. Panel in sculptured wood. Temple IV. (*Museum für Völkerkunde*, Basle.) (*Photo Mu*

me.)

intel in sculptured wood. (*Photo Musée de l'Homme.*)

[127] BONAMPAK.
Altar 1. (*Photo Giles
G. Healey.*)

[130] CHICHÉN ITZÁ. (*Photo Pierre Verger, Musée de l'Homme.*)

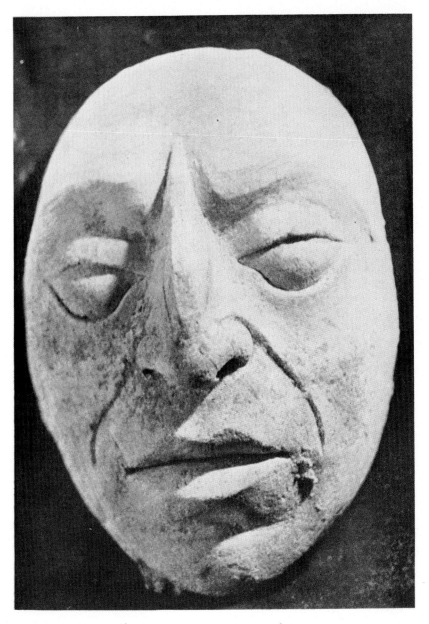

[131] PALENQUE. Stucco Head from Courtyard N—O of the Palacio. (*Photo Alberto Ruz Lhuillier.*)

[132] PALENQUE. Head cast in stucco. (*Photo Louis Limón.*)

[133] YUCATÁN.
Ceramic Whistle.
(*Photo Musée de l'Homme.*)

[134] GUATE-
MALA. Depart-
ment of Huehue-
tenango. Large
vase decorated
with a painting
representing a
religious cere-
mony. (Museum
of the University
of Pennsylvania,
Philadelphia.)

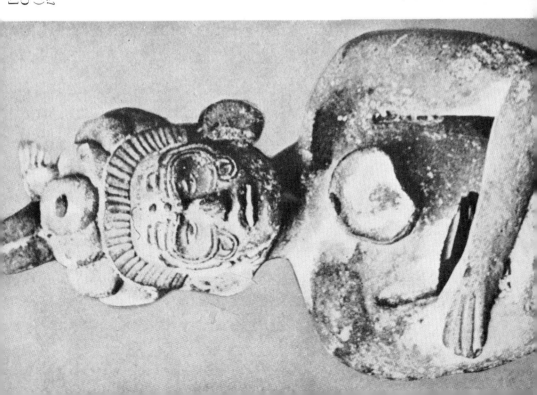

[135] PALENQUE. Mask in Relief. (*Photo Henri Lehmann.*)

[136] COPÁN. Tepen vase. Museo arqueológico de Copán. (*Photo G. Stromsvi K.*)

VI

THE MODERN MAYA

In a census taken in 1940, there were 1,957,260 Mayan Indians in Mexico, Guatemala, Honduras and British Honduras, of which 45,254 were *Wastek*. Despite the influence of the Whites and of Catholic priests, these Indians have preserved many beliefs and customs. The study of these has made valuable additions to the findings of pre-Columbian archaeology and to the accounts of missionaries and chroniclers. But the sole group which has remained completely outside white civilization is the group of the *Lakandón* who live in the State of Chiapas (Mexico) between the Ríos Usumacinta, Jatata and Lacantún. Seven small groups or *caribales* of these have been studied by J. Soustelle.[1] He has estimated that the total tribe comprises 173 individuals.

It is in the territory of the *Lakandón* that the famous ruins of Bonampak which they call the 'House of the Jaguar' (Fig. 1) are situated. This fact alone proves that there is continuity between the humble degenerate tribe in course of extinction and their great ancestors. The modern ethnology of the Mayan Indians of Yucatán, from Chiapas and Guatemala, which has perhaps been over-much neglected in favour of archaeology, would undoubtedly throw some light on those problems of a past which, despite admirable work, still has so many obscure features.

[1]Soustelle, Jacques, *Notes sur les Lakandón du lac Peljá et du Rio Jetjá* (*Chiapas*). Journal de la Société des Americanistes. Paris, new series, vol. XXV, 1933, pp. 153–80; *La culture materiélle des Indiens Lakandón*. Journal de la Société des Americanistes. Paris, new series, vol. XXIX, 1937, pp. 1–95.

Conclusion

IN concluding this exposé, which is a rapid synthesis of all the discoveries and all the progress made in the last century as a result of the explorations and study undertaken by eminent ethnologists, we must admit that the mystery of the origin of the Maya still remains unsolved. Archaeologists, by combining the results of their excavations with the very valuable observations of the old chroniclers and Christian missionaries, have been able to reconstruct the history of one of the greatest peoples of America and the various phases of a civilization of the Old World. Hitherto, however, they have not been able to relate this civilization to other American civilizations and still less to those of Europe, Asia, Africa or Oceania. Attempts to connect them have been made, notably in respect of Mayan architecture and that of southern Asia, India and Cambodia. If I mention in particular the work of Henri Marchal, from so many others, it is because this scholar had a deep knowledge of the monumental art of the two latter regions.[1]

Quite recently, Robert Heine-Geldern and Gordon F. Ekholm[2] revived this thesis, making it the principal feature of an exhibition held in one of the rooms of the American Museum of Natural History on the occasion of the Twenty-Ninth International Congress of Americanists held in New York in 1949. If certain of the affiliations proposed are spectacular, notably that between the depiction of the lotus in India and in the Mayan country,[3] it remains no less obvious that they are not sufficient to establish any degree of certainty, because the influence of South Asia can be seen neither in physical type nor in the language of the Maya. It is incomprehensible why the immigrants, who are supposed to have

[1]Marchal, Henri, *Rapprochements entre l'Art khmer et les Civilisations polynesiennes et précolombiennes.* Journal de la Société des Americanistes. Paris, new series, vol. XXVI, 1934, pp. 213–22.

[2]Heine-Geldern, Robert, and Ekholm, Gordon F., *Significant Parallels in the Symbolic Arts of Southern Asia and Middle America.* Selected Papers of the XXIXth International Congress of Americanists. Chicago, vol. II, 1951, pp. 299–328; *Parelelos significativos en el arte simbolico del Sur Asia y de Mesoamerica.* Tlatoani. Mexico, vol. II. Nos 5–6, September–December 1952, pp. 29–35.

[3]Rands, Robert L., *The Water Lily in Maya Art: a complex of alleged Asiatic Origin.* Smithsonian Institution Bureau of American Ethnology Bulletin 151. Anthropological Papers, Nos. 33–42. Washington, 1953, pp. 79–153.

imported their architecture and their art into Central America, should have neglected to introduce certain essential elements of culture, such as the wheel,[1] the bow and rice.

Other authors have always believed that the Mayan and Egyptian civilizations were connected. The existence of a hieroglyphic writing and of pyramids in the two regions appeared to them to be a proof of relationship. This thesis has now been abandoned. Mayan writing is totally different from Egyptian writing. As to the pyramids, they appear to have utterly different purposes in the Valley of the Nile and in Central America: funeral monuments on one hand, temple pedestals on the other. All the same, the discovery at Palenque, of which I have spoken in detail, proves that in certain cases the construction of the pyramid was determined by the presence of the tomb of an important personage. Its funeral character takes precedence over its religious character. But this concerns a fact which is so far unique, and does not remove the principal objection which has been made to the thesis of Egyptian influence on the Maya country, i.e. the immense difference in time which separates the building of the two monuments.

Physically, it is difficult for us to relate the Maya to an Asiatic group. 'The cranial deformation is absent from the north-east of Asia, with people who can be classed as Mongoloid, and the prominent nose with convex bridge is incompatible with the complete development of the Mongoloid physical characteristics.' 'Neither those flattened heads nor those "Proboscodean" noses are at home in Mongoloid Asia', and Ernest A. Hooton, from whom I have borrowed these phrases, adds that he is inclined to think that the ancestors of the ancient Maya were not very different from the Armenoid type from the plateaux of Iran, with hooked noses, and from the Alpine type with round heads, and that they acquired certain Mongoloid traits in their hair, pigmentation, shape of cheekbone, etc., in the course of time.

Linguistically, the Mayan language, as far as our present knowledge goes, bears no relationship to any language of the Old

---

[1] I understand by this the use of the wheel for transport of which no chronicler and no figurative document makes mention although, in very limited areas of Mexico, principally in the State of Vera Cruz, in the region of Popocatepetl, at Pánuco, in the State of Oaxaca and in the Isthmus of Panama (Coclé) small figurines in clay or metal have been found, thought to be toys, mounted on four wheels. Cf. Alphonso Caso, Matthew W. Stirling, Samuel K. Lothrop, J. Eric Thompson, Jose Garcia Payon, Gordon F. Ekholm, *Conocieron la rueda los indifenas mesoamericanos.* Cuadernos americanos, Mexico, vol. V, 1946, pp. 193–207.

M.C.–P*

World. Mayan civilization, in its very essence, retained its primitive originality over the centuries, *vis-à-vis* the civilization of the Mexican peoples. Only in the later period, that is to say, during the New Empire, did it undergo Mexican influence. From the physical point of view we can certainly find resemblances between the Maya and certain physical types from the mounds of Ohio on the one hand, and certain South American types—Peruvians, Araucanians, Charrua tribesmen, Patagonians, on the other. But these are diffuse affinities on which no certain *rapprochement* can be based.

Finally, the Mayan language, despite many endeavours, remains an independent language. We can only catch a glimpse of a link between Maya and the Mixe-Soke and Totonak languages of Mexico.

In short, Mayan civilization, until further facts are known, must be considered as the singularly brilliant result of an autonomous cultural evolution, undoubtedly encouraged by favourable environmental conditions, and engendered by a particularly fertile collective creative genius. The brutal interruption of this evolution and the annihilation of its work remain a veritable crime for which the white man bears the heavy responsibility.

INDEX

DATE DUE

NOV 0 9 2004	